I0134107

Why Men This, Why Men That?

The Truth About Everything A Woman Wants To Know

Lloyd Johnson III

© 2017 Lloyd Johnson III
All rights reserved.

ISBN: 0998560901
ISBN 13: 9780998560908
Library of Congress Control Number: 2017910906
Johnson & Co. Publishing, O'fallon, MO

To my daughter, Zione Johnson, who's the center of my life and truly reflects me.

To my genteel mother, Tracey Laron Boyd, because without her giving me those sixty minutes of reading punishments, my interest in literature may not have grown to such depths.

And in loving memory to my angel in disguise, my grandmother Sandra Patricia Johnson, who constantly encouraged me not only to reach for the stars but to go above and beyond. May you forever rest in peace.

Also, to the many women who are driven toward communicating with and understanding men. Your inspiration has been immeasurable.

Acknowledgments

Writing this book with the help and support of some of the best individuals I've encountered has been a pleasure and a gift. Without them this book may not have been written so accurately, designed so creatively, and filled with such intrigue, and for that I'd like to express my wholehearted gratitude.

Foremost, I'd like to give praise to our God almighty for the knowledge, wisdom, and strength to complete such an amazing and helpful piece of literature.

One of my dearest friends, Paris Maree Eubanks, played a major role in helping me brainstorm some of the most enticing content used throughout this book. I couldn't thank her enough.

My male and female friends—too many to name—a plethora of social-media members, bloggers, and tons of different men and women, married and divorced, all of whom in some way or another provided me with crucial information to complete such an accurate and factual piece of work.

Sincere thanks to my sister, Brienne L. Johnson, for introducing me to a phenomenal graphic designer by the name of William P. Morris. With ease, he understood my vision of what I wanted the front and back cover to represent and created an inviting final illustration I couldn't be happier with.

Finally, I'd like to give an enormous thank-you to a great friend, spiritual brother, and mentor, Darrell Lee Lloyd. Without his occasional words of wisdom and motivation, I may not have been so determined to strive for success and stay on this constant path of fulfilling my dream of writing this book and becoming an author. For that I am forever grateful.

Table of Contents

Introduction   xi

PART ONE   A REFLECTION OF HIM:
QUESTIONS AND ANSWERS ABOUT WHAT A
MAN EXPECTS, ACCEPTS, AND APPRECIATES;
YOUR INTERESTS, LOOKS, AND CHARACTER   I

1   Expectations   3
2   What He Does and Doesn't Accept   9
3   Appreciation   17
4   Pastimes and Interests   21
5   Your Appearance   25
6   Personality And Character   29

PART TWO   MEN HAVE EMOTIONS TOO:
QUESTIONS AND ANSWERS ABOUT OUR
INSECURITIES, DISTRACTIONS, CONCERNS,
COMMUNICATION, AND COMPATIBILITY   35

7   Insecurities   37
8   Distractions   42
9   His Concerns and Caring   47
10 Communication   51
11 Compatibility and Connection   56

PART THREE   THE NOT SO GOOD, THE
BAD, AND THE UGLY: QUESTIONS AND
ANSWERS ABOUT ARGUMENTS, ABUSE, HIS
CONTROLLING BEHAVIOR, AND MORE   61
12 Arguments   63
13 Abuse   69
14 Threats and Him being Threatened   75
15 Anger   80
16 Manipulation   84
17 Conflicts and Differences   88
18 Controlling Behavior   92

PART FOUR   LOVE, SEX, AND PAIN:
QUESTIONS AND ANSWERS ABOUT LOVE, SEX,
ADDICTIONS, INFIDELITY, AND DECEIT   97
19 Love   99
20 Addictions and Obsessions   104
21 The Sex   109
22 Infidelity   116
23 Lies and Deceit   120
24 Trust   124

PART FIVE   BAD TASTES IN YOUR MOUTH:
QUESTIONS AND ANSWERS ABOUT YOUR
PAST, PROBLEMS SURROUNDING YOUR CELL
PHONE, YOUR BABY'S FATHER (IF ANY), THE
MALARKEY, AND HIM CATCHING FEELINGS   129
25 Your Past   131
26 Cell-Phone Issues   136
27 Your Child's Father ("Baby Daddy")   142

28 The Malarkey   148
29 Catching Feelings   152

**PART SIX   FAMILY MATTERS: QUESTIONS
AND ANSWERS ABOUT STRESS,
RESPONSIBILITIES, EMPLOYMENT,
FINANCES, MARRIAGE, AND CHILDREN**   157
30 Stress   159
31 Responsibilities and Priorities   163
32 Employment   167
33 Finances   172
34 Marriage   177
35 Children   184

**PART SEVEN   TO BE OR NOT TO BE:
QUESTIONS AND ANSWERS ABOUT
SPENDING QUALITY TIME, LONG-DISTANCE
RELATIONSHIPS, YOUR FEMALE FRIENDS,
DATING OTHERS, SECOND CHANCES, AND
BREAKUPS**   193
36 Quality Time   195
37 Long-Distance Relationships   200
38 Your Female Friends   206
39 Dating Others   211
40 Second Chances   215
41 Breaking Up   220

About the Author   227
Suggested Titles That May Interest You   229
Share Your Thoughts   230

Introduction

As I'm lying on the couch, I hear my girlfriend's car pull into the driveway, and her door-lock system engages. She walks through the door with her cell phone glued to her ear having one of the most annoying feminine conversations I've heard since yesterday. For example, all I could hear in the background was a penetrating voice babbling about "Why men this, and why men that"—a conversation piece that I and a ton of other men get the luxury of hearing on a regular basis whether it's from eavesdropping on our girlfriends' conversations or from being victims of their millions and billions of questions and emotions.

A lot of us are victims of such instances, which is one example of why we might view women as being the most inquisitive beings on the planet, let alone the fact that they tend to ask question after question after question about us and relationships. They wonder why we act the way we do, question our motives, tactics, and schemes, and ponder if we even have any. But just because women ask, it doesn't mean men are going to tell. Some of us consider those types of questions to be intrusive and invasive, which is one of the reasons why we'll try to avoid them as much as possible. But we also avoid them because the constant questioning can become extremely tiring, and we hate having to take time out of our day to talk about things women think they already know the answer to or have already made assumptions about.

Although I understand why men have a tendency to avoid those types of questions and conversations quite often, I've learned from the many relationships I've had and continue to have with women that answering those questions and having those conversations are important to have understanding and trustworthy relationships. The sad part is that a lot of relationships are struggling or broken or don't work out because of the lack of communication. And what a lot of men need to understand is that women take pride in making their relationship "work" and understanding their man, and there's no better way to accomplish that than by focusing on communication with each other. I can proudly say that the phrase "Conversation rules the nation" is known to be true because all the communicative relationships that I've witnessed, experienced, or simply heard about have proved it, but for women, relationships, and this book's sake, let's rephrase that to "Communication helps relations." In a perfect world, all men could just be upfront and straightforward when it comes to telling women what they want, need, or desire to know about us, without holding back any secrets. But since this world isn't so perfect, I decided to become an "informant" and give up as much "confidential" information about men as you'd love to hear about.

My purpose for writing *Why Men This, Why Men That?* was to give women who are single, married, or in a relationship, all over the world, what they've always wanted—a piece of their man's brain and a taste of his thought process. The first thing I'm asked about this book is if it's written only from my personal experiences and perspective, and the answer is no. Everything mentioned in this book is well researched and obtained from men of different ages, occupations, lifestyles, and ethnicities, so you'll get to hear it all—every possibility, every perspective, every action, and every excuse there is known to man about the content mentioned. From reading this book, you'll have the ability to walk around knowing all the answers to a ton of common and not-so-common questions that you and other women could think to ask, such as, "Why a man can tell you he loves only you but still be intrigued by other women?" to "Why does he take his phone with him wherever he goes in and around the house?" and "Why does he lie about his past relationships?" plus hundreds more that are never answered, discussed, or communicated properly in relationships. *Why Men This, Why Men That?* covers almost every topic and question you could think of, so if you're curious and want to know, keep reading because all the answers are in the palm of your hand, as well as tips and solutions for each that'll help you better handle your man's actions and thoughts, for a better relationship.

Why Men This, Why Men That? is written in a simple question-answer format and includes advice sections titled "The Male Tip," so you'll be able to analyze every answer and find helpful tips about a lot of things you and other women ponder, dwell on, or ask men that seem to cause a subject change or constantly get swept under the rug. In this book, we tell you exactly what goes on through our "manly" minds in the most truthful and purest form, from expectations, your appearance, the sex, and the love to the cheating, insecurities, past relationships, opposite-sex friends, manipulative ways, the breakups, the makeups, and many more topics women desire to hear about.

So have a seat and enjoy the reasons why men this and why men that.

Part One

A REFLECTION OF HIM: Questions and Answers
About What a Man Expects, Accepts, and Appreciates;
Your Interests, Looks, and Character

1

Expectations

*M*ost men have similar expectations and assumptions about what women are responsible for in relationships, and if you ask a woman what she thinks about us and our expectations, she might sarcastically say, "Well, where do you want me to start?" For some reason, we think they're in charge of doing certain things we shouldn't have to, whether it be at home, outside, or to us physically or mentally. I'm not saying that we expect our significant other to be some sort of slave to us; I'm saying we believe that women should be in charge of certain duties that we either shouldn't be responsible for or aren't known to do. I'm sure you have an idea of what some of those duties entail. For example, household chores such as laundry, dishes, and bathing the kids are common duties we feel are more necessary for women to perform, which is why you might hear men say, "That's a woman's job." But besides typical household chores, there are plenty of other expectations we have toward women. The issue with some expectations is that they've created life-long assumptions about what we think women are or should be responsible for in our relationships. Although we think nothing cynical of our expectations, a woman on the other hand may believe some of them to be very unfair or biased, especially if she feels that her relationship is lacking a fifty-fifty effort. But whatever the case may be, women still question those expectations to this day and need answers.

1. What does he expect out of a relationship?
What a man wants and expects most out of his relationship is a woman who makes him happy. Although we may have different perspectives about the types of things a woman can do to satisfy that, the general concept is a woman who does just that—makes us happy. The way a woman acts and treats him, her credentials and interests, and so forth, are all things that can make a man happy depending on how important those qualities are to him. There are other things men expect out of relationships such as sex, love, a family, commitment, fidelity, and others, but all of them stem from the way a woman treats us and the way she provides happiness.

THE MALE TIP: Show interest in the types of things he likes and expects women to do, and do them as much as possible. It will make him extremely happy with the relationship knowing his woman puts forth effort into meeting his expectations and tries to be the best partner she can be for him.

2. Why does he expect me to cook, clean, and do so much around the house?
He might think those types of chores are mainly a woman's job. A lot of us have been raised with the impression that we go to work to pay all or most of the bills while the woman does most of the cleaning, grocery shopping, cooking, laundry, and so forth. This notion dates back from generations, and some men still perceive women as having that same type of role women had decades ago. They might expect women to act as a housewife, and cooking, cleaning, and so forth, are what that role entails. Another reason for such expectations is that some men believe that performing those types of duties will make them less of a man, so they expect women to do them. It may also give a man some sort of confirmation as being called "man of the house."

THE MALE TIP: Try to do what pleases him, but the moments you become tired or are in need of a break, simply tell him how you feel. Since men aren't known to perform those types of duties as often as women, giving you a break shouldn't be a problem no matter how unmanly he might feel washing a sink full of dishes or loading the washing machine to wash multiple loads of clothes—basically doing things a lot of men believe to be a woman's job.

3. Why does he expect me to pleasure him sexually on a daily basis?

Hopefully I'm not sounding too straightforward, but sexual pleasure is one of the many things men think women are for. It gives us a euphoric, stress-free feeling that a lot of men want, need, or don't mind getting on a daily basis, although we're not too upfront about admitting it. A man might also expect it because it gets rid of the stress and frustration caused by his job and other everyday life obstacles, and in a relationship, a woman should be that backbone to help fix or provide relief for those types of issues we experience. Another reason may be that he's addicted to the feeling it gives, and since you're his partner, you're the only one who should be satisfying that for him, and lastly, a well-known fact is that men and sex go hand in hand, and studies show we're known to have very strong sex drives, which is why we might expect that type of pleasure daily.

THE MALE TIP: Satisfy him sexually as much as possible. It's hard to lose that way. Even if he doesn't hint at it, he might just be too tired to even make a pass, but trust me when I say a man will almost never turn you down. So giving him through sex a daily dose of happiness, confidence, stress relief, and any other positive word you can think of will not hurt one bit.

4. Why does he expect me to be okay with him coming home late at night and early in the morning?

Simply put, you're the woman, and he's the man, and not too many men enjoy the fact of having a curfew after most of us have had one our whole childhood life growing up, so he might expect you to accept him coming in the house at a time that he sees fit. Also, some men feel like they shouldn't have to answer to anyone, and in this case that person is you, so he might feel like he should be able to come in whenever he wants and that it should be accepted without having to answer to you. In my opinion it's unacceptable for a man to come home during certain hours of the night or morning, but some men think otherwise.

THE MALE TIP: If you're not comfortable with him coming home during the wee hours of the night, just let it be known. Nine times out of ten, he'll understand and have more respect and caution to the situation if it's simply expressed and discussed. If that doesn't help, try finding ways to lure him home by giving him reasons why he should want to be at home rather than out and about with friends doing "God knows what."

5. Why does he expect me to be unconditionally understanding toward his decisions?

A man wants trust from his woman, and by understanding his decisions, it shows just that. He wants you to trust that he makes the right decisions and that you believe that whatever he decides to do in his life or whatever decisions he decides to make will be successful ones. The bottom line is that most men take pride in saying, "We'll handle it; we'll get it done." Therefore, we expect our woman to be understanding so we can do exactly that. If you're not going to be understanding about any of his decisions, he could very well feel like you don't trust him with making correct choices, which in turn can cause him to feel as if you're basically telling him that he's not the man who he thinks he is. Try thinking of it as if you were a parent—you may trust your children not too much in making certain decisions because they're children, and we say that they don't know any better. And giving a man the impression that you think he doesn't know any better might make him feel less of a man. So we expect our woman to be understanding and patient toward our decisions to keep that balance of who's the man and who's the woman in the relationship.

THE MALE TIP: Let him make the decisions he needs to make. If you're not understanding about some of his decisions, simply tell him why, but don't take it upon yourself to make decisions for him without talking about it first.

2

What He Does and Doesn't Accept

en go through stages of what to accept and what not to accept about their woman and about certain things she does on a regular basis, such as her attire, her acts on social media, sometimes even her choice of jobs, and all types of other things she's involved in or makes decisions about. In a relationship, it almost seems like it's just the nature of the business for a man to criticize or critique his woman and her actions, being that she's considered a representation of him, so we feel the need to let it be known what we will and will not accept. The main reason we do this is because we'd rather see you in a light or image we're satisfied with, which causes us to criticize, critique, and tell you what we will or won't accept. Some women believe those types of men to be a nuisance, but some enjoy when a man tries to mold her into what he likes. I'm sure you agree that it comes down to personal preference, but the things us men have issues about accepting and not accepting are normally all common instances within relationships.

6. Why doesn't he accept who I am, and why does he try to change me?
Perhaps he doesn't like your flaws, disagrees with certain things that you do, or he views some of your qualities and attributes as distasteful. Whichever the case, he only wants you to do some tweaking within yourself—change a little bit about you for him to view you as more tasteful, attractive, and more acceptable to him and his likings. That is why a man might try to change certain things about you, unless he's just an inconsiderate a-hole. I wouldn't see it as him being controlling, and I mention that because most of the time women believe that's exactly what it is and the only thing it could be, but I'd see it as him just trying to make sure you're everything he's ever wanted from a woman and making sure he'll be able to live with you while putting up with everything that comes with being in a relationship with you.

THE MALE TIP: You don't have to change everything about you, but try to understand and consider changing some of the things he dislikes or disagrees with about you and that both you and him will be comfortable with. Remember, relationships are a team effort, and they take sacrifices such as doing or changing things you may not want to, but it works both ways.

7. Why doesn't he accept whenever I go out with my girls, as if he doesn't like me to?

He probably gets a tad bit jealous when it's time for you to have that so-called girls' night out. Jealous in a sense of him thinking you could be doing better things, specifically with him instead of with your friends, even if it's something as simple as sitting on the couch watching television. Most men don't mind their woman going out every so often, but if you have a habit of doing it regularly or excessively, it might make him wonder if you're out being influenced by your friends and doing the wrong things you normally wouldn't do or even think about doing. It seems as if it's almost a man's nature to feel not too happy about you constantly going out because a lot of us feel you should be able to get that same enjoyable effect by spending time with us. It sounds selfish, I know, but it's just the way some men think.

THE MALE TIP: Before you leave for that girls' night out, tell him something positive that will make him feel much more comfortable and trustworthy about what you're going to be doing while you're out. Maybe even give him something to look forward to when you get back home to ease his attitude a bit.

8. Why doesn't he accept me having male friends?

A lot of men don't like or trust the idea of their woman having male friends, especially when you do things like classifying them as best friends. We don't understand what you would have to talk about or do with another guy that you couldn't do with your partner. It almost makes a man feel like he's only doing his job half the time when it comes to satisfying you in all aspects of the relationship. It could also make him feel as if you're more comfortable talking to or doing certain things around other males, which could make him feel less of a partner. The reality of it is that when men get into relationships, they feel like their woman should be able to talk to them about anything instead of having other male friends to do so. Other than that, a lot of us feel like men can't be friends with a woman without having some degree of sexual interest, which is why we don't trust the idea of our woman having male friends.

THE MALE TIP: Ditch your male friend(s). If it's hard for you to do, I'd suggest talking to them as little as possible, even if you've known them for years or they're your so-called bestie, unless they're only attracted to the same sex—they are gay, to be blunt—in which case you may get a pass to have male friends acceptably.

9. Why doesn't he accept me having social-media accounts?
Everyone knows how damaging social media can be to relationships, so it makes us cautious about accepting the fact that our girlfriend has an account. Our intuition tells us that other men are probably messaging, trying to interact with you in some way through social media, and that alone makes us wonder what goes on within those accounts and whether we can trust you. It causes us to question whether you're replying to other guys' messages and whether you're developing interest in another guy on social media, and the list goes on.

We may not come out and boldly ask those questions because we don't like to seem controlling, overwhelmed, jealous, or insecure, but that's why he may not be comfortable with you having a social-media account. We know a ton of guys use social media for flirting or trying to meet women, so we prefer our woman to just stay away from it, to avoid any altercations in our relationship. It's also known that social media can be a cause for breakups and no privacy.

THE MALE TIP: Maybe give him access to your account, even your password. Prove to him that nothing is going on negatively on your social-media accounts that will jeopardize the relationship, and don't keep it so private from him because it will cause him to think you're hiding something.

10. Why does he nitpick about and act like he doesn't accept a lot of things I do and the way I carry myself?

There's a good chance he nitpicks things you do and the way you carry yourself because he's aggravated about the way you do them. He may get tired of seeing you doing things like drinking the last bit of juice but still putting the carton back in the refrigerator with only a drop left or not leaving enough cereal for the next person to eat but putting the box back into the cabinet, or perhaps you're always making him wait on you or being late for something because it takes you an hour to do your makeup or ridiculous amounts of time to get ready. Those types of things and other instances that can be frustrating to him will cause any man to nitpick. Also, sometimes a man just nitpicks about things because he's had a bad day and just wants to complain, and I'm sure women do the same to men, so you may know exactly what I'm talking about.

THE MALE TIP: Figure out a way to fix the things he nitpicks about, but if he's only nitpicking because of a bad day, ignore it and let him nitpick away. Eventually he'll get tired of complaining like a baby. Wouldn't you?

11. Why doesn't he like or accept me being an exotic dancer, even though he met me that way?

Although he met you dancing, he probably didn't take into consideration what your job really entails right off the bat, so at the time it may not have been an issue or maybe he just didn't have any type of plans to go further than a pleasurable or lustful night with you. We know that exotic dancers get a ton of attention from men, so when we're dating one, it gets hard to grasp the fact that other men are possibly getting the pleasure of touching, seeing, or groping you all night. It's a hard pill to swallow, so after a while he may not accept it.

THE MALE TIP: Try to find another occupation to support you and your family. If you'd rather keep dancing although he doesn't accept it, explain to him how you feel about it, and maybe he will take your feelings into consideration and learn to accept it.

12. Why doesn't he like accepting new changes in my life?

He may just fear changes in life—period—not just yours. Or it may just depend on what type of change it is. For example, if it's a relocation of jobs, then there's a pretty good chance he is in fear of having to start a new life, when he already has a solid foundation of where you guys are now. If he doesn't like accepting any changes at all in your life, then he's probably comfortable where he is and doesn't want anything to mess that up or alter that comfort. Not too many men like to go through those big-change or start-over stages when they're already safe and content with their existing lives.

THE MALE TIP: Give him reasons explaining how and why those changes will not affect you or him in terms of moving backward and causing some type of difficulty or stress in both of your lives.

13. If he loves me, how come he doesn't accept everything about me?

With men, it doesn't have anything to do with us not loving you because we can love a woman and still not accept certain things about her. It all boils down to what we like or don't like about you—it is as simple as that.

THE MALE TIP: Don't be worried about him not accepting everything about you thinking he doesn't love you because that isn't the case. But if you can't get over it and need to be sure, try asking him about the things he doesn't accept about you.

14. Why doesn't he want or accept us living together?

He probably enjoys living alone because of the different benefits it has, such as the control of his own space and having his own rules without someone intervening with any of it. Or he fears that type of commitment because it's a big step in a relationship and an even bigger responsibility. Or he fears the possibility of the relationship getting worse as soon as you move in because it's known that relationships sometimes tend to go downhill as soon as a couple moves in together because of the different obstacles and disagreements that start to appear.

THE MALE TIP: Explain to him how important living together may be to you. Give him some time to think about it before forcing it. If he's the type of guy who doesn't want to live together no matter what or doesn't even consider compromising, you may need to consider moving on if you're not interested in maintaining a relationship that will never involve you moving in together.

3

Appreciation

Women do a ton of things to and for their man to show appreciation, but some men don't even realize it. Why don't they realize it? Maybe because they're too busy being selfish, only thinking about things that are important to them, so the simple acts of appreciation a woman shows goes right over their heads unnoticeable. A man who does not recognize a woman who appreciates him is simply a man who lacks something that I cannot explain. But what we do know is that when a woman gets fed up with a man for not appreciating her or recognizing the ways she shows her appreciation to him, she sometimes become very aggravated and displeased, even causing her to question whether or not she is in a relationship with the right man.

15. Why doesn't he notice and appreciate the little things I do?

He could be focused on other things that are happening in his life so much that it causes him not to notice the small appreciative things you do. Sometimes we can be so tied up in what we have going on that our attention span becomes limited, so certain things such as our woman doing small appreciative things become unnoticed.

Or he notices the appreciative things but avoids showing appreciation for whatever reasons. One reason a man might do this is because he doesn't want you to get a big head and become arrogant or conceited and become too boastful about it.

THE MALE TIP: Don't worry about him appreciating what you do or don't do. Just be yourself, and continue to do what you do no matter if a man sees it or not. It might even make you feel more confident about the type of person you are.

16. Why doesn't he appreciate me trying to push him forward in life?

Some men don't care to reach the next level or don't care for change because they're perfectly fine doing what they've been doing and are comfortable with it. Also, some men can't gather enough motivation to better themselves no matter how much you give them, or he probably feels like you're trying to pressure him into being someone or something he's not. Whatever the case, he won't appreciate you trying to push him to a better life or to do better things because he's comfortable enough with how he lives.

WHY MEN THIS, WHY MEN THAT?

THE MALE TIP: Find out what he wants out of life and focus only on pushing him toward that. If he still doesn't appreciate it, then he might not be mature enough to show it or he's comfortable enough with his life as it is.

17. Why doesn't he appreciate me constantly trying to make our relationship work?

With men, this depends on what kind of relationship it's been as well as what type of guy he is. If much of the relationship has been full of negativity, then what is there to appreciate, especially if nothing seems to change? If most of the relationship has been a good one although you guys still have issues that you're constantly trying to resolve, he probably just doesn't appreciate it out of feeling tired of you constantly having to do things for it to work. As far as the type of guy he is, every guy should appreciate a woman who tries to make her relationship work because it's the respectable and loving thing to do, and if he doesn't, it could be him being inconsiderate.

THE MALE TIP: Continue to try to make your relationship work regardless of him not appreciating it, but if the relationship seems like it will never work, you might need to consider aborting mission.

18. Why doesn't he appreciate how I go out of my way to please him?

This sounds like your classic asshole of a guy. For a man to not appreciate you going out of your way to please him, that tells other men he may be a man who lacks morals and re-spect. A real man will appreciate you putting him before yourself no matter what. He'll even find a way to return the favor or remind you that you don't have to go out your way to please him because he'd rather focus on pleasing you.

THE MALE TIP: Try to address it with him, and then give him time to start appreciating it. Do not alter your attitude be-cause of him or any other guy not appreciating something because you should always be the best person you can be to yourself and others, but start telling him how you feel if it bothers you in any way.

4

Pastimes and Interests

On a relationship, men and their hobbies go together like sponsor logos and race cars. Hobbies are very important to us when it comes to staying entertained and having something to do regularly, so when a woman is in tune with our hobbies and interests, it makes for an easier, happier long-lasting relationship. Have you noticed that one of the first questions you ask a man on the first date is "What type of things are you interested in?" That fact alone should tell you how important a man's hobbies and interests are to him. The only issue hobbies and interests have in relationships is that they're equally important to women, and I think men sometimes forget that. At times, we think our interests are more important than a woman's interests, and sometimes that gets us in trouble and causes women to question our stance and decisions about our hobbies, their hobbies, and why we act like ours are more important or why we act so selfish with them.

19. Why does he act like he enjoys the same hobbies as me when I know he doesn't?

He probably does this so that you feel like you guys have something in common. We know it's important for a woman who's interested in a man to feel like she has a few things in common with him, and if a man is interested in that woman, it can cause him to act as if he liked some of the same things she does so that he'll stay relevant to her. Some men even do it to further an agenda of trying to get something out of her since women are more willing to do things with men they like and have things in common with.

THE MALE TIP: If it bothers you, talk to him about it to make sure he knows he doesn't need to put on an act and that you'll always love and be interested in him no matter he likes the same things or not. Honesty is everything!

20. Why does he like me playing video games with him?

To some guys it's a hobby, and they enjoy video games so much that they like for their significant other to join in to experience that same enjoyment. Not only is it the experience but most importantly it serves as a bonding moment when a woman sits and plays. If you notice, guy friends become a little closer to each other when playing together, so just imagine what type of feedback he'll give you if you don't mind playing video games with him.

THE MALE TIP: Try to join in every now and then when he wants you to. If you don't have an interest in playing at all, he might even enjoy you interacting with him while he plays. Playing or not, it's a good time to bond with him.

21. Why doesn't he like the fact that I have so many (or so little) hobbies?

He may not like you having too many because it might take away the time he gets to spend with you since having a ton of hobbies can take up most, if not all, of your time. Some women have so many that it also takes their focus away from handling important priorities, which is another reason some men don't like for women to have too many hobbies.

When it comes to having only a couple of hobbies, he may not like the fact that you don't get out enough to enjoy different things or life itself. He may also not like the thought of you being a boring person.

THE MALE TIP: Whether you have too many or not enough, make sure you manage them as best as possible. Don't let your hobbies get in the way of your priorities and in the way of spending time with your partner.

22. Why does he act like watching sports is more important than what I want to do as if he cares more about it?

He may just be in a mode where he'd rather choose to do something manly than girly. A woman's hobby might not be as interesting as sitting on the couch watching the game especially on football Sunday when his favorite team is playing—not only football but whatever sport he's interested in. I speak for a ton of men when I say the feeling guys get watching a big-time game drinking a cold beer can't be compared or matched to a lot of things women like to do, such as shopping, cuddling, and so forth. But it has nothing to do with him caring more about it than you.

THE MALE TIP: Don't take it personal when he turns you down to watch sports. It's a man thing that you might not understand, but if you feel he does it too often, discuss it and try to come to an agreement to where he gets his sports but does things you want to do as well, equally and fairly.

23. Why does he want me to like and care to do things that interest him?

He may just want to be able to get along with you as best as possible, and a great way to do that is to enjoy some of the things that interest him. When a woman likes or shows interest in the same things, it brings us closer to her. Not only do we want our woman to be our relationship partner but also our friend, and most of the time, friends are friends because they get along well and enjoy some of the same things. So yes, we prefer our woman to do things that interest us.

THE MALE TIP: Try to develop an interest in some of the things he's interested in, but don't force it, and I can almost guarantee your relationship will grow stronger, more exciting, and much friendlier. Remember that friendship and togetherness are key factors in relationships.

5

Your Appearance

oday, it seems as if appearance is everything. It's basically the first thing a man recognizes. Most of the time when a man meets a woman, he will be interested to connect with her if he feels physically attracted to her. Men prefer a well-dressed woman or a woman who dresses appropriately, not a woman who goes out looking as if she's been wearing the same clothes, makeup, and hairstyle for months or as if she's desperately looking for attention. A lot of men take pride in their woman's appearance being that they're supposed to reflect each other, so when we don't agree with what you're wearing or how you're wearing it, we will have a thing or two to say about it.

24. Why doesn't he like me going out looking too sexy when I'm not going with him, as if he's concerned?

This involves a little bit of insecurity on a man's part. It probably makes him question why you need to go out looking too sexy when he should be the only man you need to accomplish that look for, so if he isn't attending your outing, he's questioning your motives. To men, there must be a purpose for you to dress that way, and one of the first things that goes through our minds is that it's to impress other men. He could also be concerned about the possibilities of other men giving you too much attention, and trying to flirt, and doesn't look forward to thinking about you dealing with things like that. Same as when a man gets cleaned up to go out and a woman's favorite remark (sometimes sarcastically) is, "Wow. Where are you going all dressed up?" or "Who are you trying to look good for?" See how that tiny notion of insecurity or curiosity passes through our brain?

THE MALE TIP: Don't dress too sexy with a look as if you're trying to replace your boyfriend. In that way, you won't make a man feel insecure. Also reassure him that nothing will happen that will jeopardize the relationship. You can even add a little encouragement by telling him you're only interested in looking that way for him.

25. Why does he joke or make negative remarks about my weight?

There are men who joke about a woman's weight thinking they are comical, and you have men who are truly serious when they speak about it. Either way there may be two differ-ent reasons. One reason is that he notices certain body parts that may need work as far as areas that need to be toned, so he jokes about them so that you won't think he's saying it in a negative, judgmental way. He's just trying to say, in a positive manner, that exercise is important to your mind, body, and spirit. Another reason is that he uses your weight as leverage to keep you down emotionally and to control your attitude. He could also be trying to make you feel as if no one else will ever be interested in you, which can give him some type of control over you if it makes you feel that he's the only guy you could ever be with.

THE MALE TIP: Try to figure out which reason it is, and act accordingly. If he does it with the intent to make your mind, body, and spirit better, then accept the criticism positively. If he does it with negative intentions, simply ignore him, and recognize that you're beautiful regardless.

26. Why does he rather I wear natural than fake?

As most men, he feels like your natural look overpowers the fake any day. Anything that alters your natural beau-ty—for example, the fake eyelashes, hair, and nails—takes away from what your true beauty really is. Men prefer to see the pure beauty in a woman rather than a fabrication of them.

THE MALE TIP: When wearing fake accessories, keep it at a minimum. Don't overdo it. Try to look as natural as possible.

27. Why doesn't he like that I don't wear underwear sometimes when I'm not at home?
He probably doesn't see a good enough reason for you to not wear panties, unless you're at home. Even though you may do it simply because of comfort, the whole thought of you not wearing panties while walking around in public could make him feel uncomfortable. He probably even thinks its skanky.

THE MALE TIP: Wear panties wherever you go outside of your home.

28. Why does it seem like he gets uncomfortable when I have a lot of skin showing at the gym?
He just doesn't want everybody looking—males, to be specific. A gym is to get some type of exercise accomplished, not to be seen having your man worry about all the attention you may be getting from those male wandering eyes. Since other men enjoy working out while looking at all the beautiful eye candy walking around, some of us don't want that eye candy to be our woman because it makes some of us uncomfortable, and by having a lot of skin showing at the gym, nine times out of ten, men are going to look. So it might make him uncomfortable, maybe even bothered, especially if he's a tad bit insecure.

THE MALE TIP: Don't go to the gym looking as if you're trying to win a sexy wardrobe contest. Instead, try to wear exercise gear that doesn't beg for attention and that doesn't try to make other men break their necks to get a peek.

6

Personality And Character

We all know personalities play a big role in getting along with others and making relationships last. It can either alter relationships in positive ways or be their demise. In the relationship world, some people say opposites attract, and others disagree, but honestly it just depends on the type of personality and character of the persons involved. I'm sure we know that a good personality is crucial toward having a long-lasting relationship, and a negative personality is sometimes hard to deal with. Fact of the matter is your personality and character are the reasons you made it as far as being in a relationship with your partner, so that should tell you how much effect it has on relationships. Therefore, always remember, no matter how much your personality differs from your partner's, how much it doesn't seem to stay in tune with his, your character will always have an impact on your life and your relationships.

29. Why do our personalities never seem to stay in tune with each other's?

Either it's by nature or because one or both of you are selfish in a sense of allowing your personalities to clash by constantly having disagreements about each other's behavior patterns or emotions or both, instead of coming to agreements or being submissive toward each other. Just like how a radio station needs a good signal to not get static, you must take turns being the good signal in your relationship to find a way to stay in tune. If this doesn't work, perhaps your personalities differ so much that it's not meant for them to stay in tune with each other.

THE MALE TIP: Try to be more understanding of his personality, and ask him to be more accepting of yours so that you both can find a way to agree to disagree about things that may obstruct personalities from staying in tune. The key to this is: understanding.

30. Why does it seem like he doesn't want to change any of his negative characteristics for me?

Either he's stuck in his ways, meaning he's fine with how he is and doesn't see a problem with it, so he doesn't want to change, or he doesn't look at you in a way that makes him want to change. Some people just need the desire to change on their own no matter how much input, advice, or opinions you may give. Some men also need to have a significant reason to want to change those negative ways, but normally being in love with you should be significant reason enough, which is what I meant by him possibly not looking at you in a way that makes him want to change.

THE MALE TIP: Give him time to change on his own or give him a reason to want to change. Sometimes we need a little boost, ultimatum, or reality check to want to change.

31. Should I stay with someone with a very different personality?

This is a choice that only you can make. Sometimes it works out fine; sometimes it doesn't. Like I've said earlier in the text, some people say opposites attract, and others disagree with that notion. It comes down to however you feel, but I'd say give him the benefit of the doubt. I'll give you a couple of scenarios. Let's say you stay in a relationship with a man who has a very different personality, but you get along perfectly fine as far as enjoying each other's company or handling business together as needed—in this case nothing is wrong. Now let's say you decide not to stay with him because of the personality difference, and later down the road, you find out that almost everything you looked for in a man was in him. Now you see where that could go wrong.

THE MALE TIP: Give it time to understand the personality differences, and see what you can and can't deal with. If what you can't deal with overpowers the things you can, that may

LLOYD JOHNSON III

be a sign it's probably not going to work out. If the things you can deal with overpower the things you can't, then you should be perfectly fine sticking around.

32. Why does he have a problem with my character suddenly?

This one's tricky. There could have been issues about your character in the past that he didn't necessarily agree with or took a liking to, but he accepted them because of whatever other interest he had in you. And if those issues are still present, he could've finally decided to address them, so it may not be "suddenly"—he may just finally have decided to address the issues he's had about your character. Or he's just starting to unlike certain things about you, maybe because he has a different outlook on life and what he likes about a woman than he had in the past.

THE MALE TIP: First off, keep in mind that him suddenly not liking your character isn't your fault, so don't take the blame. But if you want to keep up, meaning change as he changes, just find out what he dislikes and work on bettering those qualities but mainly bettering your entire self for the sake of your own personal growth.

33. Why doesn't he see me as wifey material?

Many factors can play a role in this situation. It could be because of your sexual history with other men, the type of things you've done in the past, how you act as of now, the fact that he can't take you to meet his mom, and so on, because these are things that only some men base their decision off when thinking about marrying, so it varies. We men have a certain idea or expectation of what a wife is supposed to be and how she's supposed to act, and if his expectation of that doesn't fit your personality, then he might not consider you wifey material. We base the decision of labeling a woman wifey material on whether she's a good woman overall and a good woman who fits our individual needs and sometimes on her track record, or past, as well, which in my opinion shouldn't be involved because the past should stay the past, right?

THE MALE TIP: Work on being a woman whom he not only sees as great but a woman whom you see as great as well. Find ways to prove to him that you're what he wants, needs, and would love to have as a wife, and I'm pretty sure his wife is what he'll ask you to be.

Part Two

MEN HAVE EMOTIONS TOO: Questions and Answers about our Insecurities, Distractions, Concerns, Communication, and Compatibility

7

Insecurities

ot only are women filled with a plethora of insecurities, but men are as well. We may not seem to have as many as women, but we have just as many, if not more. We have similar types of insecurities in terms of the types of reactions within our relationships, for example, having insecure thoughts about going out with single friends or about what was going on while out past 1:00 a.m., and so forth. One thing for sure is that we might try not to make our insecurities seem so obvious because to some of us, it's not the manly thing to do. We may show it, although oftentimes we may not. In any case, we don't want to look like a softie in the relationship, which is why we choose when to express what we're insecure about. An essential point is that men do have plenty of insecurities, and most of them are only expressed when they begin to influence our thoughts, emotions, and relationship.

34. Why does he seem insecure when I decide to go out for a drink or simply go out—period?

He's just worried about the things that could happen while you're out. For example, conversing and becoming attentive toward another guy and then ending up making a mistake that jeopardizes the relationship. Just the thought of something like that worries us, and we know when a woman goes out, it makes situations like that more likely to happen, so it probably just makes him a little worried. To say it bluntly, he doesn't fully trust your actions and doesn't want you to go out and mess up.

THE MALE TIP: Reassure him that there's nothing to worry about. You could even call him here and there while you're out to do so. That will at least make him feel a little more comfortable about the situation.

35. Why does he act insecure when I tell him I need space?

He might fear you're possibly losing interest in him and never coming back. Normally, when a woman asks us for space, we immediately think she wants to end the relationship or that she's lost interest, and saying she needs space is just her way of giving us a polite excuse to leave. So we act insecure because we fear the possibility of you eventually losing interest or moving on and losing you altogether.

THE MALE TIP: If you need space, communicate with him and explain why you need it, and let him know it won't alter any positive feelings you have toward him or the relationship. Reassure him that it's only temporary and that you're not going anywhere.

36. Why is he insecure about sex?

He probably has doubts about himself being able to satisfy you, and the doubts could come from him thinking his penis is too small, or perhaps you're not giving him a positive, enjoyable display of pleasure during sex, which can cause him and other men to feel like they aren't doing enough in bed. We take pride in our sexual performance, so if we're not receiving some type of positive feedback or reaction that tells us we're doing great, it can cause us to doubt that we're satisfying you, and we begin to think we're doing something wrong, which in turn turns into insecurity.

THE MALE TIP: Tell him he's great; give him positive feedback regarding his performance, through communication and display. Interact with him as much as possible during sex.

37. Why does he still act insecure about the things I tell him he's great at?

Either he's the type of person who's always going to be doubtful of himself, no matter what you or someone else tells him, or he acts that way to make sure everything he does is still good enough. All men want to make sure their woman is satisfied and pleased, especially with things we put effort into, and instead of sounding emotional by constantly asking questions such as "Is it good enough?" we might act a little insecure just to find out.

THE MALE TIP: Continue to tell him he's great at the things he's insecure about. He's probably just the type who enjoys or needs to hear it.

38. What makes him feel insecure about my friends and me hanging out with them?
He probably thinks they might be a bad influence on you. A lot of men believe women are easily influenced by their friends, which sometimes becomes an issue. If he doesn't trust them, it's because he thinks they are or could be influencing you to do certain things you shouldn't be doing such as making bad decisions that can affect the relationship, especially while you're hanging out with them. The simple thought of it causes us to be insecure toward your friends.

THE MALE TIP: Make sure he knows you don't let any of your friends influence or encourage you to make bad decisions. That should take away some of the insecurity he has toward your friends.

39. What do I do that makes him feel insecure about our relationship?
Not dedicating yourself to the relationship or not putting effort into things that couples should do together such as hanging out, conversing regularly, traveling, and making decisions together, and so forth, are things that will make a

man feel insecure about his relationship. If you're not doing things like that, it could make him feel like you're not taking the relationship seriously, and it may not feel like a real relationship. Another possibility is if you're not treating him like a true partner by not taking his thoughts and feelings into consideration or doing things that make him feel like your partner.

THE MALE TIP: Take him and the relationship seriously. Show him that you mean business and want the relationship just as much he does.

8

Distractions

oesn't it seem like it's in a man's nature to be distracted while conversing with women? A lot of times it's the smallest things that distract us—from something on TV, a random thought popping up in our head, or a simple daydream. Whatever it is, it causes women to complain and ask that famous question, "Are you listening to me?" It's true that sometimes men don't have an interest in talking about certain topics women love to talk about, which is one excuse or reason we get distracted. I bet some men agree that they'd rather be playing a video game or watching football than hearing their woman speak about flowers she went to look at in the department store. This and many other examples are proof that men being distracted while conversing with a woman is nothing close to rare.

40. Why does he get distracted seeing other women walk by?

I'm sure women know men have issues controlling their lustful thoughts, which pretty much sums up the answer. For example, a man can see an attractive woman walking by, and no matter what's going on around him, he'll get distracted by wondering what it'd be like to satisfy whatever lustful thought he has in his mind. The good thing is, in a sarcastic way, he's not trying to fall in love with her just by looking; he's only trying to get a peek of her physical attributes that may be attractive to him while satisfying his lustful thought or two in the process.

THE MALE TIP: Understand that a man is just being a man, and consider letting him look from time to time because honestly something like this can only be fixed if a man has the desire to fix it. No matter who you are, it's hard not to pay attention to things we deem attractive, so try not to take it personally.

41. Why is he easily distracted when I'm telling him something important?

To you it may be important, but to him it may be the last thing he's worried about or interested in. Women are passionate about certain things that men aren't passionate about at all, and sometimes the reason we're so easily distracted when you're telling us something important is because we may not think it's important at all. If it's a topic most people know for a fact is important, and he still gets distracted, then he's just being human. People get distracted all the time.

THE MALE TIP: Figure out what topics you both think are important. Converse with him about what you feel is a must-hear, which should help him to be more in tune without getting distracted whenever you're telling him something important. If he still gets distracted no matter what, then you may just need to repeat what you say to make sure he heard you, but be patient with him, and understand that distractions are a part of human nature.

42. What makes him so distracted to the point where he accidentally calls me another woman's name, especially during sex?

I hate to be the harbinger of bad news, but during intercourse or not, if he calls you by another woman's name, it normally means he's thinking or fantasizing about another woman, or his mind just got sidetracked, and he called you by someone's name that he's talked to that day or a woman who he's had a past with. If you're wondering why a man will fantasize about another woman, it's either because he misses her if they've had great memories together or it's a woman whom he's attracted to or interested in having sex with. Fantasizing is all about imagination, and it can cause us to be so deep in thought that we accidentally call our partner by the name of the person we're imagining.

THE MALE TIP: Address the issue as soon as it happens. If it's done during intercourse, maybe try finding new ways to spice it up so that he thinks of, enjoys, and imagines only you. That way he doesn't need to imagine another.

43. Why does he purposely distract me when I'm getting ready for a night out without him?

The essential point is he doesn't want or like you to go anywhere, or he does it playfully to hold you up. When men would rather their partners stayed at home or did something with them instead of going with friends, they may get the tendency to distract their partners a bit to try preventing them from going anywhere. You might have that friend who's waiting for you or a certain time you need to be somewhere, and we know that distracting you can possibly interfere with those plans so that we get what we want—for you to stay home or not go anywhere with friends.

THE MALE TIP: Tell him you'll be back as soon as possible and try to give him something to look forward to you coming back. That might even make him help you get ready since the sooner you leave, the sooner you'll be getting back.

44. Why does he try distracting me when I want to talk to him about sentimental things?

Either he does it when he's not in the mood to talk about sentimental things or he's the type who's very alpha male and doesn't have an interest whatsoever in talking sentimentally. Having sentimental conversations makes some men feel distraught or feminine in a sense, and they'll do whatever it takes to avoid those types of conversations, which in this case is by using distractions.

THE MALE TIP: No matter how sentimental it is, if it's an issue that's important for you to talk about or get off your chest, let it be known, and he should fully understand. But also take his feelings into consideration and respect that he may not like having those types of conversations sometimes. Choose your battles.

9

His Concerns and Caring

Women often wonder why we don't care or seem as concerned as they are about certain situations or discussions sometimes. For example, when you're telling us about you wanting to switch shifts at work or about what happened in the latest episode of *Orange Is the New Black*, we may not seem to really care because those types of discussions may not be as important to us as they might be to you. The sad part is that sometimes we act like we care to make you feel better, but in the back of our minds, we couldn't care less. Now this doesn't pertain to all men because some of us care about everything you say, but many of them really do play the role. As far as our concerns, I'll say we choose what to be concerned about no matter whether it's something we're supposed to be concerned about or not.

45. Why isn't he ever concerned as I am about the important things in our relationship?

One of the main reasons men don't like to be concerned with some of the important things in a relationship is because some of those things cause stress and other issues, and a lot of us prefer to leave as much stress behind as possible. The bills not being paid on time, the family pet becoming ill, or the kids not being able to get everything they wanted for Christmas are a few situations that a man will try not to be concerned about because although those things are important, they can be heavy burdens and cause a ton of stress when we're concerned about them. We simply prefer to live a life that involves little or no concern rather than a life full of it.

THE MALE TIP: Let him handle his concerns how he sees fit. Try not to make it a big issue, and understand that even though men don't act concerned at times, most of us truly are—we're just trying to block the potential stress and disappointment that comes from it.

46. Why does he make it seem like he doesn't care about my feelings?

If he does it intentionally, he may just be trying to agitate you for whatever reason. Maybe you've made him mad or acted like you don't care about his feelings, so he's doing it out of spite or by way of revenge. Another reason, which I hate to say, is that it's possible he truly doesn't care about your feelings, but let's hope that's not the case. If he does it unintentionally, he may just be the type of guy who has a hardcore persona and doesn't know any other way to act other than tough, so it's possible it might seem like he doesn't care, but he does. Even if he's not hardcore, it's probably just his personality that comes off as not seeming to care.

THE MALE TIP: Let him know when you feel like he's being insensitive or inconsiderate toward your feelings. Communication is important when discussing each other's feelings.

47. Why isn't he concerned about me telling him I need a vacation?

A lot of times when a man hears "I need a vacation," we immediately assume that a woman is only hinting at having a lot of things going on in her life, and all she's really asking for is a break from it all. Although you say it, we don't take it literally because it's used so loosely nowadays. For example, some women use it as a sarcastic remark to give the notion that they have had a long, tiring, and stressful day at work. Women also use it as an excuse to want to get away from their current situation they've had to deal with unwillingly that may have caused them some type of stress or strain in their life or relationship. The term being thrown around so loosely these days causes us not to be concerned after hearing the "I need a vacation" speech. We just don't take it as seriously as you might actually mean it.

THE MALE TIP: When telling him you need a vacation, inform him how serious you are, and speak with sincerity. Maybe even research trips together to show you're serious.

48. Why doesn't he seem concerned about what I'm going through in my life?

He could also be going through things in his life, which makes it difficult to be concerned about another's. We understand how important it is to be involved in our partner's life and all the trials and tribulations she might undergo, but understand that everyone has his or her own concerns and battles to deal with, which may be draining and make being concerned with another's unmanageable. The worst-case scenario is that he doesn't care what you're going through because he's the self-centered or inconsiderate type.

THE MALE TIP: If you feel it's important for him to show some type of concern, explain that to him, but understand that it's possible he has a lot to worry about himself. So try not to force your burdens upon him. Men are always concerned about whether their partner is happy or not, although sometimes we just have a funny way of showing it.

10

Communication

Relationships are built on communication. Without some form of it, whether it be written, visual, verbal, or nonverbal, there wouldn't be any opportunities for us to develop relationships. Good communication is important and extremely necessary to have healthy relationships. Unfortunately, a man not communicating issues properly is one of the main concerns and problems women have in their relationship, which is one of the main causes of their relationship not progressing. We forget how important it is to have and focus on good communication no matter how much it can be the demise of our relationships. Why do you think that is? In my opinion, there's so much that goes on in our everyday lives that we get sidetracked and forget the importance of certain things— such as focused attention and communication with our partner.

49. Why is it so hard for him to communicate with me?

Sometimes it's hard for any man to communicate in ways that satisfy a woman because the way women want or need to communicate is sometimes much different than the way men like to. This is partly because of the different masculine and feminine characteristics men and women have. A lot of times we get the impression that when a woman wants to talk, there are going to be plenty of feminine feelings involved, such as tenderness, sympathy, maternal instincts, and several other emotions of that nature. I'm not saying men don't have the same type of feelings, but I think they're more commonly displayed by women. A lot of us prefer to avoid those feminine feelings, and that's one of the main reasons it may be hard for him to fully communicate with you. Another possibility is that he's the type of guy who hasn't really learned how to communicate. Some men naturally have a hard time communicating because of personal reasons, or maybe they never learned how to communicate effectively.

THE MALE TIP: Converse with him about the importance of communication in your relationship. Be aware of your tone of voice, and make sure you discuss it in an inviting tone, not an antagonistic one.

50. What makes him avoid talking about things I feel are serious and important?

Men normally do this when they're not in the mood to talk about those types of things, or if it's a topic that frustrates us, we'll sometimes try to avoid talking about it. It just depends on what's being discussed because there are plenty of reasons why he and other men avoid certain conversations. But whatever personal reason a man has, the bottom line is that he is not in the mood to talk about it.

THE MALE TIP: Let him avoid it until he's in the mood to talk about it. If it's something you think cannot wait and needs to be discussed or resolved, inform him how important it is and that it needs to be dealt with ASAP.

51. Why does he act like he wants me to be in the dark about certain things?

He might feel like you don't need to be involved in everything. A lot of us have a perspective of being able to handle things on our own, without any help, involvement, or having to discuss it with our partner. The funny thing is that we know it's not the right attitude to have in a relationship but continue to do it. And because we act this way, a woman will feel like she's in the dark about certain things. It's much more satisfying for us to handle it like a man, meaning doing things ourselves in a stereotypical masculine manner, away from any femininity. The good news is that he's probably not keeping you in the dark purposely; he might just prefer to handle things on his own without needing to discuss anything. If in fact he is doing it purposely, it may be things he thinks you're better off not knowing about.

THE MALE TIP: If you hate the feeling of being kept in the dark, tell him exactly how you feel. It may change or it may not—it all depends on what type of guy you're dealing with. Be understanding of his personality because it might be something you must accept, if it never changes. However, he should change because communicating with each other is important in relationships.

52. Why doesn't he like communicating with me about our differences in our relationship?

Either he feels like he doesn't need to converse about it because they'll end up working themselves out, or speaking about it might add negative energy to the conversation or relationship depending on how defensive you guys become. Have you ever noticed that when couples discuss their differences, it becomes an argument because it seems like both parties become very defensive trying to convince each other who's the problem? Knowing this, some men prefer not to discuss their differences since it could make things worse, when they could just let it go and avoid any arguments or negative energy it may bring.

THE MALE TIP: When discussing differences, do so as cordially as possible. Avoid becoming defensive and argumentative.

53. Why doesn't he care to communicate with me regularly about simple things like how he feels or how his day went?

He's probably not the type who likes to converse about things like that. I can relate if that's the case because sometimes I just like to come home, relax, maybe watch a movie, or talk about the kids, not about my day. This attitude might even be common for men because there isn't much need to talk about how we feel or how our day went when we're more concerned about whether our woman is okay. In a sense, he may not want you to worry about him so much because what matters most is how you're feeling. Some of us also don't like discussing our day if it's been a rough one and prefer not to relive it by talking about it, especially when in a bad mood.

THE MALE TIP: If you can sense him not wanting to talk because he's not in a good mood, either console him or give him time to cool off before trying to converse with him about how he feels or his day. If he's the type of guy who doesn't like communicating at all about those types of things, tell him how important those conversations are to you, or simply let him be.

11

Compatibility and Connection

aving a connection and being compatible with each other goes hand in hand with having a great satisfying relationship. It's the foundation of any type of relationship people develop with each other. How many times have you've heard of two people who have never had some type of connection or feeling of compatibility with each other building a relationship? If you have, it's rare because no one builds relationships without one or the other anymore, especially when there's so many different ways people can connect and be compatible with each other. For example, connections range from many physical or spiritual forms, which some of us refer to as vibes, and compatibilities range from things like agreeing on issues or decisions together, sharing the same values, or sharing similar likes or dislikes, and much more. These days experiencing one or the other is imperative when it comes to choosing the right partner to develop a relationship with.

54. Why does he think we experienced a connection and are compatible after only one date?

He probably likes to moves fast and felt like all he needed was one similarity with you to make him feel compatible. A lot of men agree that once we find a woman who has something in common with us, we feel connected, even after only one date. It could be something as simple as both individuals favoring the same sports team or having a similar outlook toward life. There are many things that can cause a man to feel a connection or that you're both compatible with each other, but it depends on the mind-set of that particular man. It's also possible for a man to be physically attracted to you or want you so much that he forces a connection where he acts like there is one although there isn't, similar to the way a man lusts.

THE MALE TIP: Find out what he thinks make you compatible with each other, and let him know if there are not enough factors to decide that you are compatible with one another. Also, if you feel that it takes more than one date to figure out whether you're compatible or not, discuss that with him.

55. Why does he feel like we need to hang out more after we've found a connection?

He wants to develop a stronger connection. Most of the time after a man finds a connection with a woman, he feels that's when the fun begins, meaning it's time to start doing more things and spending more time together to develop more connections and make them stronger. To put it in a common perspective, it's like after the first time a woman has sexual intercourse, she wants to explore different positions, pleasures, or body parts to get a better understanding or connection with herself or with her partner. It's pretty much the same concept with men wanting to do more with a woman after the first initial connection.

THE MALE TIP: Do more with him. It won't hurt to find out how many different ways you connect with him.

56. Do I make him feel like we're not compatible because I always answer with an "I don't care" whenever he asks me to do something he likes?

It can depend on how often you answer with "I don't care." If it's constantly, he might begin to doubt how compatible you two really are. We know it's common for women to answer with "I don't care" or the most famous one "It doesn't matter," but when it's done excessively, we might feel like our relationship lacks true compatibility. Although all men can't relate to this notion, some of us don't think anything of it after hearing answers like "I don't care" or "It doesn't matter." We'll just accept it and continue on with our day, without any other thoughts about it.

THE MALE TIP: Try not to answer with an "I don't care" or "It doesn't matter" too often. Mix it up by actually deciding on

things so that you don't create the impression that the relationship lacks compatibility.

57. Why does he say and act as if there's nothing there when we seem to get along fine?

There could be a few reasons why that statement is implied,
depending on the guy's reasoning or motives. From most experiences, it's because he's not interested in you as you might
be in him. Women do the same to men, and it's normally a
woman's way of telling a guy he's in the friend zone, meaning
there's nothing there, or will be, other than a friendship.
Men pretty much do the same thing. It's our way of saying
we're okay with having you as a friend without looking at you
for any other relationship because he may not think you're
compatible with him.

THE MALE TIP: Ask him for the specific reason why he feels
that way, only if you need closure. If you're still interested in
more than a friendship with him, understand his reasoning,
and try to change it in order for him to start seeing you as
someone he can be in a relationship with.

58. Why does he still want to spend time with me after we established we're not compatible and never made a connection?

Normally this means he's still trying to develop some type
of relationship with you. If the dating is fresh, meaning in
the beginning stages, or if he's physically attracted to you,
he might still want to date to make sure he's not missing

anything as far as being compatible in some type of way. The bad news is that he could have an ulterior motive to get something from you, copulation for example, so he tries to spend as much time as he can with you in hopes of accomplishing that.

THE MALE TIP: Pay attention to and question his motives to make sure he wants to spend time with you for the right reasons. If you deem it unnecessary to continue spending time with him being that you're not compatible, discuss it with him respectfully. Let him down easy.

59. Why does he think we're not compatible just because the sex isn't good?

For men, sexual connection is very important within relationships. In this day and age, it could either make or break your relationship. When your partner thinks you're not compatible because of the sex, it normally means he thinks the relationship wouldn't last because the sex isn't good. To a lot of men, good sex is mandatory.

THE MALE TIP: Find ways to spice up the sex. Try new things, new positions, new toys, videos—whatever you can get your hands on. If that doesn't work, understand that some people just don't connect sexually with others. That's life.

Part Three

THE NOT SO GOOD, THE BAD, AND THE UGLY:
Questions and Answers about Arguments, Abuse, His
Controlling Behavior, and More

12

Arguments

Arguments are common in all kinds of relationships, and to some it's an everyday facet in relationships. Some men and women would even go as far as saying a relationship wouldn't be normal without any arguments. I'm sure all of us notice how much we argue about the smallest things, without contemplation. Is it because we love the small taste of battle and becoming the victor, or do we just love to voice our opinion and prove to be correct? Whatever the reason, it's like an everyday chore to some couples and a bad habit that's hard to get rid of as if it's been instilled into our character. It causes hurt, grief, sorrow, and negative energy to enter our relationship and our well-being. We have to ask ourselves how long we will let it be a source of troubles to our relationship or how long before we find a new approach or method to get our point across without rhubarb.

60. Why does it seem like he enjoys arguing daily? What exactly does it do for him?

It may make him feel in control, having the upper hand, and a lot of men enjoy that feeling. It could also make him feel relieved if it's an issue that's been bothering him, that he's been wanting or needing to get off his chest. The reason he might like to argue daily or all the time is because he might enjoy the feeling he gets from it so much that it makes him enjoy arguing, or it could be because he feels the need to keep addressing the problems or differences you guys have to make sure a solution is being found. Although a lot of us men seem to pick an argument about the smallest things, I think I speak for a lot of us when I say we don't really like to argue—it's just our way of expressing our mind.

THE MALE TIP: Avoid any unnecessary arguments as best as you can to keep them at a minimum because excessive arguing may eventually lead a relationship to ruin.

61. Why is it so hard for him to let go of arguments?

Of course, he has to have the last word in the argument—most men do. When we don't, it makes us feel like we've lost the argument. One of our natural instincts is competitiveness, so we don't like to lose, even when it comes to arguments. Not only do we not like to lose, but we also don't like letting go of an argument that hasn't been resolved yet, so sometimes we'll argue until we get our points across or until whatever is we're arguing about has been resolved or understood. Also, some guys just like to hear themselves talk, and they'll go on and on and on, no matter what.

THE MALE TIP: Let him have the last word, and then maybe he'll put a sock in it. If that's too hard for you to do, then try making him feel as if he's either won or found a solution, or just agree to disagree. I'm sure one of those ways will make him let go of the argument, unless he's the guy who likes to go on and on and on, no matter what. That's someone you just have to ignore.

62. Why does he get so aggressive with me after arguments?

Arguments may create steam, fury, aggravation, frustration, or anything else of that nature, which will cause a man to get aggressive. Men don't really have an on and off button that they can press to control their frustration in an instant, which is why the term "calm down" is commonly used during or after arguments. Since we can't really control it, it may take a while for that aggressive attitude to die down, which is why men still act aggressive after the initial argument. He's just still frustrated.

THE MALE TIP: Find an amicable way of calming him down. You can do that by keeping the energy of the situation cordial and giving him time to cool off. In other words, take the subtle approach and be nice.

63. Why does he think I'm supposed to be nice just because he's ready to, after an argument?

A lot of us feel that if we've dropped the argument by letting it go and acting amicable afterward, then our woman should do the same because there's no point in her continuing on with it acting incongruous or in anger. Therefore, we expect a woman to be nice when we're ready or have decided to after an argument.

THE MALE TIP: Advise him that just because he's ready to act cooperatively or nicely, it doesn't mean you're obligated to. But the right thing to do is surrender, forgive, and move on. Negative energy from arguments isn't good for any relationship.

64. Why does he argue with me about certain household chores?

He may get upset and argumentative when you approach him about certain household chores that he thinks are your responsibility. Like I've said earlier in the book, some men feel that women are responsible for certain household chores that a man isn't, like the laundry, dishes, folding clothes, and so forth, and when a man is asked to do them, it could either make him upset, argumentative, or both. If that's not the case, he might just dislike doing them, so he creates an argument to avoid having to.

THE MALE TIP: Approach him about doing certain chores as if you're simply asking for help, not being demanding. You could also figure out which chores he doesn't like doing and come to an agreement on who does what.

65. Why does he get louder and louder during arguments?
It's his way of trying to get his point across. If a man's arguing with a woman, and she persists after he's made his point, it will cause him to feel as if she didn't hear or understand him, which will make us get louder and louder so that you do hear us. Getting louder is sometimes our way of saying that we've said what we needed to say or to stop prolonging the situation because it only makes us more frustrated when a woman continues to argue, especially after a point has been made. Also, for some men and depending on what type of argument it is, getting louder is just their method of relieving some anger or stress.

THE MALE TIP: As he gets louder, tell him you understand where he's coming from. Console him. If it's just his method for relieving anger, then find or suggest other ways to help him relieve his anger. Some men and women have said make-up sex works great. But if he's out of control, loud, and angry, you may need to walk out of the room or house before it escalates into something more serious.

66. Why doesn't he stop arguing until I start crying?
For whatever reason, he may have begun to feel sorry, sympathetic, or he just doesn't like to see you cry. When a woman starts crying because of an argument or something we've said, it can make us compassionate or dissatisfied with ourselves and will make us want to stop arguing. This is simply because

when a woman cries, it normally means she's been hurt or disappointed in some type of way, and most of us don't like seeing a woman express those types of feelings through tears, especially if we're at fault.

THE MALE TIP: Express to him through conversation when you feel hurt, disappointed, or anything else of that nature before beginning to cry.

13

Abuse

Abuse can be described as a pattern of behavior mainly used with the intent to control, and it comes in many forms. It's a common issue within relationships, and some would even consider it a disease, being that it has so many effects on the abuser, the abused, and the relationship itself. I wouldn't be surprised if it's one of the main causes of damaged relationships and of damage to one's health and well-being. The three most common types of abuse women experience within relationships include physical, sexual, and emotional abuse. Each type of abuse is used for the same purpose: to control and to manipulate. A ton of women are or have been a victim to some form of abuse during their lifetime, so it's safe to say almost every relationship will encounter some form of it at least once.

67. What makes him put his hands on me, especially after I tell him things he doesn't like or want to hear?

He could be frustrated or aggravated with you and does it to make himself feel better, sort of like a stress reliever, unfortunately. Another reason is because he might feel it's the only way for him to control your actions. When it's done after hearing something such as a negative remark or something he gets emotional about, it just means you may have pressed his button, which caused him to act or react abusively.

THE MALE TIP: Try not to incite or provoke him during times of frustration. Avoid confrontation as much as possible. If the abuse begins to become constant or serious, either leave the situation or call for help. But be sure of your decision when involving a third party.

68. Why does he think physical abuse will control me?

Most men believe it to a certain extent, but to be specific, physical abuse can cause fear, and fear controls the way some people act or respond. It's the same concept of disciplining a child, so to speak. In relationships it's a man trying to use physical abuse as a way of disciplining or controlling you. For example, once he feels like you've gotten out of line, out of control, or that you took a situation too far, especially during an argument, he may feel as if resorting to violence is the only way to control you and tranquil the situation.

THE MALE TIP: Don't allow him to hear, think, or see that physical abuse has some type of control over you because he might make it a habit in doing so.

69. Will he ever stop abusing me?

It's very much possible, but it's up to him to do so. Two things have to happen in order for him to stop. One, he may have to see or understand that abuse gets him nowhere besides having to experience consequences. Two, it has to be in his heart to want to stop. If a man is comfortable abusing you, and it's working to his advantage, rarely will he feel the need to stop, but once he sees that it doesn't work or that it does more harm than good, eventually he should stop. It just depends on his mind-set and what you allow to happen.

THE MALE TIP: Do not tolerate physical abuse. Explain that it accomplishes nothing besides having negative effects on the relationship.

70. Why does he try to mentally abuse me?

It's just another way to control your thoughts, actions, or feelings. Some men mentally abuse women by degrading them, labeling them as fat, dumb, ugly, worthless, and so forth, to make them lose their self-respect. And some men use manipulation, by saying deceitful things so that she'll believe anything and everything he says, which will allow him to be in control. However he does it, it's simply to get what he wants from you.

THE MALE TIP: Don't let him control your thoughts. Block out the fictitious remarks and live with an enlightened, positive mind-set regardless of the demeaning remarks directed toward you.

71. Does he hit me on purpose or by accident?

He may do it purposely or accidentally. If he does it purposely, then obviously his intentions were not good. If he does it accidentally, it was only a reaction to your action without thinking. For example, if you both were involved in an intense argument and you were to resort to violence first, his reaction of physical abuse may have just been natural or accidental, or perhaps his emotions got the best of him.

THE MALE TIP: Ask, but either way, it isn't acceptable.

72. Does he even think abusing me is wrong?

He may or may not. If he's a man of respect, nine times out of ten, he'll know it's wrong, but if he's a man lacking morals, he may not understand or think about the damage it does to your mind, body, and spirit. It all depends on what type of guy he is. Is he a man of respect or a man who lacks morals?

THE MALE TIP: Converse with him about how he feels or what he thinks about it. If he thinks it's wrong, he's right; if he doesn't, you may have to consider your next steps regarding him and your relationship.

73. Does it mean he doesn't love me if he abuses me?

Just because he abuses you doesn't mean he doesn't love or care about you because there could be a few reasons why he abuses you, or like I've said before, sometimes it's accidental, but it has nothing to do with loving you or not. Men do crazy things all the time whether we love a woman or not, and sometimes we act without thinking things through no matter who or what it affects, so abusing you doesn't have anything to do with love. Some men will even say they abused you out of love, but don't listen to that—it's the most farcical thing I've ever heard.

THE MALE TIP: Understand that men sometimes do things without thinking, so don't doubt his love because of abuse. Instead, converse with him about it to get him to understand the importance of thinking before acting and the effects abuse has on you and the relationship.

74. Do men feel secure in physically and mentally abusive relationships?

It depends on the circumstances. If the man is the abuser, he may feel secure from being or feeling in control or feared by his partner. When speaking of a relationship where both individuals are considered the abuser, some men won't feel secure because of knowing or believing that a woman will eventually call it quits, ending the relationship, as well as knowing abusive relationships aren't known to last forever.

THE MALE TIP: Converse with him about how, when, and why he should and shouldn't feel secure in an abusive relationship.

75. How does he feel after I use violence on him?

He may feel disrespected or violated in a sense, or he may feel perfectly fine, meaning he thinks nothing of it. For example, there's the type of guys who feel the same as some women being physically or emotionally hurt, betrayed, disappointed or anything else of that nature, and then there's the type of guys who don't feel anything and who simply think of it as a woman just releasing anger resorting to violence, so it depends on the type of guy you're involved with.

THE MALE TIP: Discuss with him how he feels about you resorting to violence and take his feelings into consideration.

14

Threats and Him Being Threatened

In relationships, men use threats to accomplish their motives, control situations, and create fear or intimidation in their partner. Although different threats have different purposes, in relationships you hear the same kind of threats for the same reasons. For example, some men will threaten to break your things, some will threaten to break up with you, and some will threaten you with violence—all to get what they want. I'm sure that you as well as other women have been victim to a threat at some point in life, which is why it can be considered a common or recurrent problem that should be addressed. Furthermore, not only do men provide the threats, but they too are threatened in many ways, which sometimes isn't even noticed, but the fact of the matter is that threats are very much alive within relationships.

76. Why does he threaten to break up with me when things get bad?

This threat is used by both men and women and is probably the most common. One reason a man will use this threat to break up with you is in hopes of you changing the bad happenings into good. This means that if things aren't or haven't been going well in the relationship, he may think threatening you will change that. It basically serves as an ultimatum and some men believe it to be very effective. He might also use this threat when you're not living up to his expectations or standards and is his way of letting you know there are things within you that need to be fixed or improved. Finally, I'm sad to say, it's used as an easy way out from having to deal with any problems.

THE MALE TIP: You could try to improve the things he wants improved and turn whatever negatives he sees in your relationship into positive. But at the same time, inform him that threats shouldn't and will not be tolerated in your relationship.

77. Why does he threaten to break my belongings when he gets angry from us arguing and fighting?

One reason is that it's his way of relieving some of his aggravation while arguing and fighting, the same way some people get angry and throw or break things because it helps them relieve tension or frustration. Another reason is to try to get you to settle down or be calm during an argument since threatening to damage someone's valuables can possibly control their attitude and the situation. Arguments cause emotions to run high, so they make it hard for people to get their point across, and anger grows quickly. All these factors can be detrimental to a woman's attitude, causing her to act aggressively and violently, so a man will threaten to destroy the things he or you feel are important to you in hopes of mellowing your attitude or the situation. However, sometimes it only makes matters worse. This threat is also used simply as a display of anger.

THE MALE TIP: Don't show him your belongings mean a lot to you. If he already knows they mean something to you, discuss the importance of those valuables and that damaging them might only make matters worse. Don't let him see that that threat works because he might continue to use it in future arguments.

78. Why does he still threaten me when he sees it accomplishes nothing?

He's either doing it to satisfy his own ego and emotions, or he thinks it still aggravates you although you don't show it. He may also feel like it works to his advantage and helps accomplish whatever motive he has because sometimes things will bother or weigh on us no matter how much we try to ignore or show it having no effect on us. It's just human nature.

THE MALE TIP: Continue showing that his threats don't accomplish anything, and consider conversing about it.

79. Why is he threatened by my success?

If he's threatened by your success, I'd say he's just worried about your accomplishments exceeding his. Do you remember the "man runs the house" mind-set or cliché I talked about earlier in the book? I believe it ties into the reason a man is threatened by a woman's success. Since we believe it's mainly our job to provide for the family as far as paying bills and making sure the family is financially stable, when the role's reversed because of a woman's success, some men may get a little threatened by that. It can make a man feel as if he's below you, or it may make him feel like the family relies on you instead of him, and for a man that's a hard pill to swallow. Men aren't known to enjoy having conversations about how their partner or spouse makes more money than them.

THE MALE TIP: Continue to make him feel like he's the provider, supporter, and in control of the manly duties. Although it sounds stereotypical, some men still have that type of outlook about relationships. Also, don't rub any of your success in his face, and most importantly, don't hold yourself back from any success because of him.

80. Why does he act threatened by me having a kid?

Believe it or not, some men are threatened by a woman's kid because of the responsibility it entails such as taking care of the kid—teaching, watching, spending time, disciplining, and so forth—and even more responsibility if he's not the biological father because of the extra things he may have to deal with. You having to put your kids first when it comes to priorities is sometimes an issue for certain men. There's also the possibility of you having to deal with the biological father, and some men consider that to be a big threat being that it makes communication with each other very open and possible for wrongdoings. Also, the thought of your kid being the deciding factor of whether the relationship lasts or not poses a threat. There are so many things that can change or become complicated in a relationship when a child is involved, and all of them make a man feel threatened.

THE MALE TIP: Reassure him that he should never be threatened by your kid for any reason whatsoever, and encourage him to think about the positives instead of the negatives of the situation.

15

Anger

On relationships, anger can be a huge issue and is something we all experience or have experienced throughout. It's a problematic issue being that a lot of people handle their anger incorrectly. Few men handle their anger quietly, while a lot of us are known to handle it in ways that are perilous to our relationship. We display anger through different tones of voice, sets of actions, or different types of body language, all in obnoxious types of ways. And being that anger mainly has negative effects on people's relationships, it's an issue that needs to be handled appropriately when necessary, and situations that involve anger need to be addressed to understand a man's logic of why he gets angry or upset about certain situations and incidents within relationships.

81. Why does he get angry with me over nothing?
It could be that he's just in a bad mood and decided to take it out on you. For example, something that happened in the day that had nothing to do with you could've made him angry or caused him to have a bad day, or you've done something unpleasant to him recently or in the past, which maybe he was reminded of that caused him to become angry. Or he's just disappointed in you for whatever reason. Each one of these scenarios can definitely cause him to express anger toward you since they are means of triggering negativity.

THE MALE TIP: Converse with him about why he's angry, and remind him that being angry at someone when he or she is not the cause is unjust and unacceptable.

82. Why does he get so angry about me not being on time?
Almost every man gets angry or upset at a woman when they're going somewhere as a couple and the woman's the hold up because there shouldn't be any reason for it. As a couple, some things are routine, and going out together is one of them, so when you're late or holding a man up, he might feel like you're being insensitive and inconsiderate, causing him to become angry. As men, we understand how long it takes for a woman to get ready, but when it causes you to constantly not be on time, it will make a man upset.

THE MALE TIP: Be considerate and on time as much as possible.

83. Why does he get angry when I buy food but don't bring him any?

Because it's inconsiderate. When you're in a relationship, if you bring food home you're almost obligated to bring your partner food as well. Coming home with food only for yourself may give the impression that you're selfish or don't care whether he eats or not, and in relationships men feel that a woman should be considerate when it comes to things like that. Remember the saying "The key to a man's heart is through his stomach." Think about how you'd feel if he were to bring food home only for himself, especially when you're starving.

THE MALE TIP: Grab food for him also. He'll appreciate it whether he's hungry or not.

84. Why does he get angry when I try to talk about our problems?

A lot of times problems will cause aggravation, frustration, or anger, so when a problem is mentioned or discussed, it may cause a person to display those same types of emotions. Some men would rather not talk about their relationship problems to avoid the negative emotions that may come with it. He may also have a short temper, which will cause him to get angry about discussing something he doesn't want to discuss or discussing something that involves differences.

THE MALE TIP: Try waiting for the right time to discuss it. If there's never really a right time, you may have to reconsider dealing with a man who has that type of attitude. Try discussing problems with an optimistic attitude so he won't get too defensive or agitated about it.

85. Why does he get so irate when I say no to sex?

Men knowingly obsess over sex more than women, so if he asks for it and you tell him no, chances are it will make him upset since he didn't get what he expected. The fact that a lot of men think sex is important in relationships and can even make or break a relationship should make it understandable why he and other men might get angry when it's not available, especially when it's unavailable because of a woman declining. He could also need that sexual fix so badly that it makes him mad when he doesn't get it.

THE MALE TIP: Try to please him as much as possible sexually or in other ways. If you think it isn't necessary to always give, converse with him with the intent of getting him to understand how you think and feel about the ordeal. If that doesn't work, he may need to seek professional help because he might have a strong addiction for it, which could be a problem or cause problems within your relationship.

16

Manipulation

Manipulation is a tool used by both men and women. It's defined as a skillful tactic used to handle and control a situation or an individual. By men, in relationships it's commonly used to get what we want—control the situation—which is done in many different ways. A lot of times, manipulation is unnoticeable, but to some, it's very much conspicuous. I believe the image of the word is viewed as devious, deceitful, or unscrupulous but it's not just limited to negative connotations because it's also used in many different positive ways. It all depends on one's intentions or objectives. If his intentions are good or altruistic, then he may manipulate you in a positive manner to do positive things, but if his intentions are bad and egocentric, then his manipulations may be aimed toward negative, cynical acts. Some would argue that it's mostly used in self-ish ways rather than benevolent, but whichever the case, manipulation is very much alive within relationships, and some men are in the driver's seat partaking in it.

86. Why does he manipulate me to do certain things and act certain ways toward people?

He's satisfying his agenda, trying to mold you into the person he wants you to be by having you do things that will satisfy him and others, or he could be trying to figure out if he has control of some of your thoughts and actions. For example, if he wants you to do something you may not be interested in, such as watching a football game with him on television, he may use manipulative tactics to get you to watch it, or if he's around a certain group of people who have high standards different than yours, he may manipulate you in ways to make sure you act as if you had their same high standards or similar ones. When a man manipulates a woman just to see how much control he has with her thoughts and actions, there's a good chance he's playing mind games or is preparing to use those manipulative ways with bad or selfish intentions, and that's a man you need to be aware of because it can be very damaging to you and the relationship.

THE MALE TIP: Pay attention to the different ways he tries to manipulate you to be aware of his intentions. Never allow a man to manipulate you for any negative or wrong reason that may be damaging to your inner self or your relationship.

Also, inform him that manipulation isn't needed; all he must do is communicate.

87. Why does he manipulate me with love?

Men do this to have control or an advantage over women. When a man shows a woman that he loves her, she'll do a lot of things for him, even things that she normally wouldn't do if he wasn't in love with her. We know how important that "love" word is to a lot of women, and many things can get accomplished in a man's favor when it's used. It could be something he wants or hidden motives he has that cause him to manipulate your feelings, sometimes making you feel like he truly loves you when maybe he doesn't. A lot of men use this method more than you think, but it doesn't mean he doesn't love you at all.

THE MALE TIP: Pay attention to his ways and actions, especially to make sure you know his feelings are authentic when he says or shows he loves you.

88. Why does he manipulate our sex?

He may need to do so for you to be pleasured, such as making false seductive noises or overexaggerating the feeling of intercourse, like what women are known to do. He could also do it as a way of pleasuring himself with whatever fantasies he might have. For example, visualizing sex with someone else while having sex with you, or imagining doing other kinky things you may not do or are never interested in. It's sort of like when a woman imagines herself sitting on a beach sipping her favorite drink although she's at home sitting on the couch—it's just a way to manipulate your mind into more pleasurable circumstances, which is why he and other men manipulate sex sometimes.

THE MALE TIP: If you feel it's not acceptable for him to manipulate the sex, then you must converse that. If you don't see a problem with it, let him enjoy the imaginable pleasures, so it can stay just that—an imagination.

89. How do I know if I'm being manipulated?

It's very hard to tell. There's normally no evidence that will show whether he manipulates you unless he blatantly tells you. The only way to know is to pay attention to common signs that might point to it. Signs such as him giving you a gift so now he feels you must return the favor by doing something for him; if he responds with remarks like, "You don't really love me" after arguing about things you never do for him, or if he uses sexual coercion in any way. These and other common signs will at least give you an idea of whether you're being manipulated.

THE MALE TIP: Pay attention to different signs of manipulation in relationships such as him making you feel guilty for everything, making you doubt yourself, and making you want what he wants. If they're used constantly or selfishly, then there's a good chance you're being manipulated. If all else fails, ask.

17

Conflicts and Differences

Many would agree that it'd be a beautiful thing if there were relationships without conflict or relationships without off-the-wall differences, but almost every relationship has one or the other, if not both. Some people view it as a good thing because they believe it helps keep the relationship new, different, or as they say, "It keeps the fire burning" since it's believed that opposites attract. Although the words "differences" and "conflicts" are perceived with mostly negative connotation since they mainly cause negative reactions, confusion, or harm to relationships, they're not only limited to negativity. Differences and conflicts can be associated with positivity as well, being that experiencing or overcoming them sometimes helps the relationship. Just think about how many times you've conflicted with your partner, and hours later you understood each other more or began to take each other's feelings and thoughts into consideration.

90. Why does it seem like he must conflict with me about everything?

Perhaps he enjoys conflict, he's one of those men born with an always grumpy attitude, or he has to be right about everything, which will make him conflict about everything. Or maybe there was something disrespectful you've done to him in the past or present that causes him to have a grudge or attitude toward you. It's also true that some people give off a negative type of vibe or energy, which can naturally cause others to dislike or conflict with them. I'm sure you've met someone whose attitude rubbed you the wrong way before.

THE MALE TIP: Converse with him about the importance of minimizing conflicts in your relationship—too many conflicts can become damaging.

91. Why does he like me so much even though we're so different?

This is because your attributes, interests, or characteristics that are different from his probably add spice, passion, and excitement to his life or the relationship. Sometimes we men have needs or desires that are never met or fulfilled because our personality may not allow it, and a woman who's different can encourage us to meet those needs. This is one of the reasons why the term "opposites attract" is deemed truthful.

He could also like the fact that you're different if he's never had a successful relationship with a woman who has the same type of personality as he does.

THE MALE TIP: Make sure he likes you for legitimate reasons for a successful long-lasting relationship, not just for the moment.

92. Why does he act different around his friends?

A lot of men get around other men and feel as if they have to prove themselves by being macho, ballsy, and full of testosterone, when it normally isn't their way of acting when around only their partner. I know sometimes it's distasteful, annoying, offensive, or even weird, but that's just the way some men decide to show their manliness or male chauvinism to their friends. In simpler terms, some of us act more sensitive around our partner, but once we get around our friends, that sensitivity diminishes, which will cause us to act a little different.

THE MALE TIP: Let him do what he needs to do around his friends, but if his actions toward you are obnoxious, annoying, offensive, or negative, let him know it needs to stop and that it's disrespectful or embarrassing. But try not to create a scene about it.

93. Why is there always a difference in what type of movies or TV shows we like to watch?
This is just both of you having different interests in what you watch.

THE MALE TIP: Try being interested in what he likes to watch. Also try getting him interested in what you like watching.

18

Controlling Behavior

For women, speaking about a man who's controlling is sometimes a very touchy subject because of the different emotional and psychological symptoms they experience from it such as stress, concern, fear, anger, embarrassment, guilt, anxiety, and many more. Although dating a controlling man is mainly frowned upon, on a good note it has its positives, but that depends on how you view them. Some women see them as attractive and helpful, some view them with disgust, and some view them as a mixture of both, based on how much and what type of things men try to control. For example, situations such as where you can and can't go, the way you dress, and the type of friends you hang around are common situations men try to have a little control over and are situations that some women either like or dislike a man to control. I'm sure you agree that almost every woman who's been in a relationship has been victim to a man who has tried to control something, but the question is why.

94. Why does he try to control me?

There are a few reasons why. He could be the type of guy who enjoys domination over women, he could feel responsible for keeping order and stability in the relationship, or he wants his wishes to be your command. I'd also say most men have a natural instinct of wanting to be the commander or head of household, which means they control it. Sometimes it's nothing personal—it's just a man's quality.

THE MALE TIP: Don't allow him to control you in a negative manner. If he tries to control you using aggression or physical abuse, I'd suggest leaving the situation or defending yourself. If it gets too serious, suggest that he seek professional help. But mainly, only allow him to control what doesn't affect your livelihood or well-being.

95. Why does he try to control where I can or can't go?

It's mainly an insecurity issue. Normally when a man tries to control where you can or can't go, it means he's fearful or worried about what might happen that could be damaging to him or the relationship. For example, the possibility of you going to a club and interacting with another male or you hanging out with a female friend who dislikes him are situations that can cause negative thoughts or insecurities about you going because of the issues that could result from it. It could also be fueled by a bit of jealousy, which causes thoughts such as him thinking you might have a good time without him or you finding interests elsewhere and in other people whom he may not approve of.

THE MALE TIP: Try to have a mutual agreement with him on what places are acceptable and unacceptable to attend—clubs, bars, parties, strip clubs, and so forth—as well as how often, but don't allow him to have too much control over it because you might miss out on life's enjoyments.

96. Why does he try to control how I dress?

Mainly because he doesn't want you looking unnecessarily seductive by showing too much skin or too many curves, or he wants you to portray a certain image around his friends, family, or loved ones. Some men take their woman's attire personal, meaning they feel their woman should dress to their liking or standard. If a man thinks that a woman dresses too seductive, it could make him feel insecure about whether she truly loves and respects him since dressing that way while in a relationship can send a misleading message to other men, at least from our point of view. We prefer to be able to describe our woman as classy and respectful in the way she dresses. If he's the type who likes his women to dress sexier, it's either because he wants them looking more fabulous than any other woman, or he's in love with the way she looks in that type of attire.

THE MALE TIP: Dress appropriately at all times and try to make sure your partner is comfortable with the way you dress. If he wants you to dress sexy at times, consider it because it may actually have a positive effect on the relationship. Also, although you have to consider his thoughts since you're in a relationship, remember that you still have to dress for you first.

97. Why does he want me to stay home while he goes out to parties?

There may be things that go on at parties you may not approve of or be happy with. For example, interactions with other women, which is rarely unavoidable at parties, or things that you didn't know he was into such as heavy drinking or wild partying. If that's not the case, he may just want some time to hang out with his buddies every now and then.

THE MALE TIP: If it's not important, just stay home, and let him enjoy himself. If it's something that bothers you, address it. But keep in mind that trusting your partner is essential to healthy relationships.

98. Why does he constantly blame me for everything?

It's a technique some men use to make a woman feel guilty, weaken her, and implement and disguise control over her. When some women feel guilty or at fault for something that happened in her relationship, nine times out of ten times, she'll try to do everything in her power to make it right or make amends, which causes her to be more susceptible in pleasing and granting her man's demands; this gives him an advantage or slight control over her in a way, although she may not notice it. The blame game is basically played to get the upper hand. It's also possible he blames you to make himself look good as if he doesn't make mistakes or is God's gift to women, as some would say.

THE MALE TIP: Accept blame only when you're truly at fault, and don't allow yourself to be blamed or frowned upon for every single incident in your relationship.

Part Four

LOVE, SEX, AND PAIN: Questions and Answers about
Love, Sex, Addictions, Infidelity, and Deceit

19

Love

ove has many different meanings, definitions, and connotations, but I believe the best description is an intense feeling of deep affection, romance, or even sexual attachment. Throughout our relationships, we experience at least one, if not all, of those feelings, and most would agree they aid for stronger, longer-lasting relationships. Once it's included in our relationship, doesn't it seem as if our expectations become higher, our commitments become a little more promising, and the passion and intimacy between each other grows stronger? Not everyone loves the same, but the qualities we display toward love are similar. The drawback is that we're known to love differently than women as far as how we display our feelings, how we react in different emotional situations, how we set

emotional boundaries, and how we have different perceptions of what true love is. It seems as if there will forever be
confusion about what men think true love is in relationships, but once you understand and accept the fact that a
lot of us are naturally prone to not show as much love as a
woman does in different circumstances, you may begin to
understand why we do certain things, good or bad, even
though love is involved.

99. Why is it so hard for him to say "I love you"?

Hopefully not, but he could be afraid of commitment. Since
love is such a strong word, once you tell a woman you love her,
it seems as if she gets even more emotionally attached, causing
her to want a more committed relationship. Some men fear or
want to avoid that type of relationship or commitment, which
makes it hard for a man to say the words "I love you."

If he's in a committed relationship with you already, there
are other possible issues such as him not wanting to seem weak
in a sense of having to express so much emotion, fearing you
don't feel the same way or being afraid of getting hurt by you
taking advantage of him after he tells you he loves you.

THE MALE TIP: Encourage him to feel comfortable using the
word "love," or just be patient, and let him say it when he's ready.

100. If he loves me, why does he do things that he knows will hurt my feelings?

It may not be intentional. A lot of times when a man hurts
the woman he loves, it's just because of the type of mood he's

in, and it's nothing personal. For example, when we act out of anger, we're not thinking about the consequences or how our actions will make our woman feel, which causes us to hurt feelings unintentionally, no matter how much we love someone. If a man does it deliberately, he may do it to be vengeful or get under your skin, meaning he's trying to annoy or irritate you for whatever reason. The good thing is that it has nothing to do with him loving you or not—it's just something we do at times.

THE MALE TIP: Understand that it may not be intentional or anything personal, and try not to be so vulnerable toward his negative actions. Remember that it has nothing to do with "love."

101. Why does he love his mother more than he loves me?
I'd say, "He's just a mama's boy," meaning he's excessively attached to his mother with a tremendous amount of love. Some men view their mom as the most important woman in their lives, which can naturally cause them to show their mother more love than they do their partner. If he's not a "mama's boy," then it could stem from how he was raised. He may have been taught such things as to always treat his mother with utmost respect, to always care for her, and to never let her down, and those types of lessons can cause him to show his mother more love than you. Sometimes a man can show his mom more love than his partner although he doesn't love her more, but I believe it has something to do with the fact that his mother is and has always been in his life.

THE MALE TIP: If you feel that it's unacceptable or unhealthy for your relationship, talk to him about it, and tell him how it makes you feel because it may cause him to put more effort and emphasis in showing you more love than he shows her.

102. Why does he try to avoid PDA (public displays of affection)?

Because showing his affectionate side might make him nervous, uncomfortable, or even anxious. Some men just don't like others seeing them do things that should mainly be done in private, and a man who prefers privacy prefers to keep his relationship discreet. There's also the possibility of him being too macho to show his soft, mushy, loveable side in public. Also, depending on the extent of your relationship, it's possible he avoids PDA because he doesn't want to be seen dating you.

THE MALE TIP: Allow him to have his privacy. If you feel that disliking PDA is a serious issue for him, then try making him feel as comfortable and accepting about it as possible. Also, try keeping it to a minimum.

103. Can he love me forever?

Yes, a man can love you forever, but "Will he?" is a question for which the answer may change. A lot of factors are involved for a man to love you forever. Factors such as whether you're worth it, how well and how long you've been acquainted, what type of relationship you have, and so forth. He must have a reason to want and be willing to love you forever, unless he's what I call "crazy" and loves you for no reason. Be heedful though; it's very possible for a man to tell you that he'll love you forever but ends up thinking otherwise later down the line.

THE MALE TIP: If you want him to love you forever, give him reasons to, but don't expect any man to so that you'll avoid possible disappointment or confusion.

20

Addictions and Obsessions

ike drugs, relationships and other things can be just as addicting. There can be things within your partner he may be addicted to that are difficult for you to cope with and damaging to your relationship. Things such as going to clubs, parties, watching pornography, having intercourse, or him being obsessed with his career are all things a man may find addicting. Although there's a ton of addictions a man can adhere to, I'd say most men adhere to these same types of addictions and complications within their relationship. The biggest issue is dealing with those addictions while trying to maintain a healthy long-lasting relationship. Like others, if you have no idea where to start, try examining each addiction, understand why the addictions are present and give him such a euphoric feeling, and then begin thinking of ways that will help satisfy his addiction or ways that will help him cope with them. Whichever you choose, remember that it's best you first understand why he's addicted to such things before deciding what action to take. Understanding makes things much easier.

104. Why does he seem addicted to hanging out and going to clubs?

There are several possible reasons why, but I'd say the majority act addicted because they still feel the enjoyment of that type of lifestyle. The meeting of new people, the party atmosphere such as the music, dancing, and possible flirting, or alcohol consumption may still be entertaining to him. It's also possible that he may not be happy at home or with the relationship, so he goes out to enjoy himself and fill that void of not being happy at home or to take his mind off a damaged relationship. Another odd reason, which sometimes happens, is that he wants to be able to do what his single friends do or what he used to do back when he was single, which is go out whenever or wherever he chooses.

THE MALE TIP: Try making yourself and your home more enjoyable to be around. Give him something to look forward to as much as possible. It may just keep him home more often.

105. Why is he addicted to watching porn even though he has me for sexual pleasure?

Research shows it can be caused by things such as psychological disorders, depression, childhood trauma, visual stimulation, the quick fix, and the fact that it's so readily available. If he doesn't have any type of disorders and none of the depression or trauma factors pertain to him, then I'd say he's addicted to the quick-fix porn provides. It's so much easier to choose a satisfactory porn video or browse the many different titles and features an adult-entertainment website has than to deal with the many possible issues a man's partner may come with. So, although he has you for sexual satisfaction, viewing porn just comes with so many different options to choose from that are also satisfactory as well as it being easily accessible.

THE MALE TIP: Find more ways that will satisfy his needs and desires without the use of porn. After doing so, if he's still obsessed with pornography, it's probably just a personal issue within him, and he may need to seek counseling.

106. Why does he seem more obsessed with his career than with me?

He probably feels that his career is his top priority, for whatever reason. Also, being that some men are so career driven, which he may or may not be, it's possible that it causes him to be obsessed with it. Once a man becomes obsessed with his career, a lot of his focus and time are put into it, and the time spent with his partner and others becomes limited, therefore making you feel like he's more into his career than into you. His career might also bring him more joy in his life than anything else.

THE MALE TIP: Converse about it, tell him you understand that his career is important to him, and remind him that family and relationships are just as important, if not more. If nothing changes, it might be a personal issue that he himself must come to realize. Some men won't realize it's a problem until problems within their relationship persist because of it.

107. Why is he so obsessed with me wearing perfume to bed?

That means he loves for his woman to have a distinctive yet pleasant smell in bed. It can make him feel attracted all over again while serving as an ingredient for arousal. If you didn't know, a lot of men prefer their woman to go to bed wearing that "scent of a woman"; it puts us in a good mood while making us comfortable.

THE MALE TIP: Wear the most amazing and sensational women's fragrance you have to offer, or wear the fragrance he prefers. It will be much appreciated.

108. Why does he act so obsessed with me?

When a man is obsessed with the woman he's in a relationship with—you—it means he loves and admires almost everything about you. From the way you walk and the way you talk to your scent, your eyes, and your curves—basically everything. There may be a ton of other things I didn't mention that he loves about you, but that's why he's so obsessed—because of what he loves about you. You could also be filling some type of void he's been missing in his life, which is another reason why a man will act obsessed with a woman.

THE MALE TIP: Think of his obsession as positive since it's merely a compliment, but if it causes any type of relationship issues or he becomes overbearing, address it before it becomes a strain on both of you. You could also try giving him other things to focus his attention on because obsessing too much can become dangerous.

21

The Sex

For men, having sexual intercourse in their relationship seems just as important as having a spine. It has many positive effects and medical benefits not only in the human body but in your everyday life as well. Some consider it overrated, but I'd say it's mainly praised by both men and women in the most loving and exciting relationships. It may be more important to men than it is to women, which probably has something to do with human physiology, by us having more testosterone and aggressive hormones. Since this may be the case, it's probably one of the reasons we look at sex as a regular necessity. For men, not having enough intercourse can cause us to experience anger, frustration, mood swings, doubt, and so on. A lot of women are knowledgeable of this and make it a point to keep their man satisfied with some type of sexual

activity regularly. The bad news for some is that sex too often can have negative effects, such as losing interest in the
sex, causing your partner to feel drained, or causing the
relationship to feel like it's based on sex. But whether positive or negative, women have a plethora of questions about
us and sex.

109. Why doesn't he make sure I'm satisfied while having sex?

He's just being a bit selfish, or he doesn't know how to satisfy
you during sex. A lot of men need to understand that sex
is much more than just male penetration, male dominance,
and male orgasms. It's kissing, touching, feeling, arousing,
emotional, exciting and pleasurable for both man and woman. At least that's how it should be. Since a lot of men don't
understand the importance of this concept, they end up satisfying only themselves during intercourse.

If he notices you're not satisfied and doesn't try doing so,
there's a good chance he's careless and is only concerned with
getting personal satisfaction.

THE MALE TIP: Mention it to him. Also, try adding more
foreplay and different sex positions that will arouse both of
you. Hopefully he gets the hint.

110. Why doesn't he take his time to make it feel like it's more than just sex?

Either he's the anxious type when it comes to having sex or he
doesn't have the finesse, flair, or knowledge to understand
the importance and effect patient sex can have on a woman.

Every man doesn't have sex the same way—there are different styles, motions, techniques, and so forth. Your guy might enjoy or prefer a hurried technique, and he might assume that's the way you like it. The worst-case scenario is that he thinks sex is just sex, without any meaning or emotion behind it.

THE MALE TIP: Tell him exactly how you feel about it. The good thing is that it can be fixed and adjusted.

III. Why doesn't he ever want to have foreplay?

He probably likes to get straight to the point or doesn't understand or realize how important foreplay can be for women during sexual encounters. Some men understand that it's intimate, loving, and euphoric and can spice up their relationship and sex life, so they enjoy performing it, but there are also men who aren't as sexual and who may not understand or know how or where to even begin using foreplay. Other men think it isn't necessary. Let's just hope the reason isn't that he's just a boring guy when it comes to having sex.

THE MALE TIP: Teach him the importance of foreplay and the positive effects it can have on you, your sexuality, and your relationship. You could also show him what you like and how it's done.

112. Why isn't his sex as passionate as it was in the beginning of the relationship?

It may not be as exciting as it was in the beginning. In the beginning of relationships, men try to make sure the sex feels as romantic, passionate, sensual, or exciting as possible for reasons such as keeping him and you intrigued, attracted, and satisfied with something to talk about. Then, as time goes by in the relationship, that effort from him may slowly deplete because he may not feel the need to be as passionate as he was since he's already proven what his sexual performance can be, or he feels it's not as necessary as it used to be since you have sex on a regular basis as a couple. Sex in relationships sometimes becomes and feels routine, which is a cause for men to not put so much effort and passion into it every time. The worst reason possible is that he's lost a bit of love or care toward you and the relationship.

THE MALE TIP: Try not to make sex feel routine. Give him something to look forward to when it comes to sexual intercourse. Try new things. Also, make sure he still looks at you in the same loving, caring, and compassionate way as he did during the beginning of the relationship.

113. Why does it seem like he's uninterested in having sex with me?
For whatever reason, he may not care for you as much as he used to, which can cause him to lose interest in the sex, or the sex may be unexciting or unpleasurable. Also, another possibility that shouldn't be ruled out is that he could be sleeping with another woman, so his interest and focus is elsewhere.

THE MALE TIP: Either converse with him about what caused him to be uninterested or try different things that can spice up your sex life to try keeping him interested.

114. Why does he act like sex is so important in our relationship?

A lot of men and women think sex is important in relationships. With men, it's something we tend to focus on, which might be a primal thing, but the fact of the matter is that we love it for several different reasons. For example, it can help relieve stress, it allows us to feel connected with our partner, and has so many other health benefits as well as making us feel positive about ourselves and our body. Also, the whole aspect of a man connecting to and penetrating the woman he loves, satisfying her at the same time makes it one of the most pleasurable feelings a man can experience in his relationship. Those types of feelings and benefits can make sex very important for men. He could also just be a sex addict and be obsessed with having sex.

THE MALE TIP: The only solution for this question is to ask him.

115. Why does he always hint at wanting to have a threesome?

If he's never experienced one, he may just want to feel what it's like, but if he's already had one, it's probably something he enjoys doing. For the record, there are men who have never got to experience what a threesome feels like and only hear about them through other people's experience or through pornography, and then there are men who have a freaky sexual side and have experienced it at least once and enjoy the feeling they get from it. He could also be testing you only to see what you're willing to do for him.

THE MALE TIP: Find out if he's already experienced one, and ask him if a threesome is something he really wants. Consider trying it out once, but if you have no aspirations to try it or refuse to have one, tell him exactly what you think about it and how it might make you feel if you went through with it. We already know it's often frowned upon.

116. Why does he discuss our sex life to his friends?

Normally, it only happens when the topic of discussion is sex and it's only gossip. We discuss it to get things off our chest that bother or excite us. He could also be gossiping about it to compare or make his sex life sound fantastic to his friends, but again it's mainly discussed because it's an interesting conversation piece among men. And you know what they say—men gossip just as much as women do.

THE MALE TIP: If you don't like your partner discussing your sex life with his friends, inform him. Those types of secrets should stay between you two and shouldn't be discussed, unless you're okay with it.

117. Why does he act like he has a problem using protection/condoms?

It's mainly a feeling issue. Almost all men know that using protection through condoms can take a lot of the physical sensation away, so they might try to avoid using them. Another reason could be that making him use protection after you've been together for quite some time could make him feel like less of a boyfriend or like you don't trust that he hasn't been having sex with other women, preventing STDs, or you don't trust that he's reliable enough to prevent you from getting pregnant by pulling out or away from your genitals before ejaculation.

THE MALE TIP: If you prefer him to use protection, let him know you're just not ready to have sex without it. Also, remind him how important it is to use protection and that it has nothing to do with not trusting or disliking him. If it does have to do with you not trusting him, just be honest about it.

118. Why does he want oral sex so much?

It's just something he likes. The different mental and physical emotions oral sex provides can be very satisfying, and he may be addicted to those feelings. Oral sex can truly make a man feel like he's on top of the world, or it can make him feel like his woman is deeply in love with him being that receiving oral sex without protection is more of a special act to a lot of people. And those special acts can have lasting effects on men causing us to enjoy and want it more and more.

THE MALE TIP: Try performing it on him as much as possible. If it's something that disgusts you or something you don't care to do, try telling him, even though hearing it might disappoint him.

22

Infidelity

These days, infidelity seems like a common issue, and some would even say it's the norm. It causes many negative emotional effects and is very damaging to your relationship, possibly causing the end of your relationship. It's frowned upon, as it should be, but the sad thing is that a lot of men don't frown on it enough to focus on avoiding it. It's as if men don't care to look at it from a woman's point of view, and the woman is normally the one who ends up devastated by her man's infidelity, but if we were to look at it from a woman's perspective and think about how damaging it is to a woman's spirit, I believe there would be less instances of infidelity from men. A lot of questions and discussions are stirred around the causes of infidelity in men, which are mostly similar from men's points of view.

119. What makes a man cheat?

A man will give a plethora of excuses for why he cheats, but no matter the reason, excuse, or testimony, the initial problem lies within him. Some men find themselves cheating because they want something new or their partner doesn't show enough love, respect, gratitude, or affection, so they begin looking for it in another woman. I hate to say, but some men get bored or tired of the sex or relationship with their partner and look for fulfillment and excitement elsewhere—through another woman. Some men cheat because they like the thrill, they think they won't get caught, or they feel like they can do whatever they want. Another possibility that is rare is that he cheats simply because he's insecure and wants more security of having a "backup plan (woman)" available in case you decide to leave. A lot of men just want to have their cake and eat it too.

THE MALE TIP: Consider taking him to counseling for his infidelity issues since it's truly an issue within himself no matter how many excuses he gives, and there are no justifications for infidelity. You could also try conversing with him about it to find a solution yourself, which I'd say will be very hard to do but worth a try if you care.

120. Can I stop him from cheating?

Yes and no. There are ways to minimize it like being the best woman you can be for him, but I don't believe there's any way to fully stop a man from cheating. The issue lies within him.

THE MALE TIP: Suggest he seek counseling, and do everything you can to be the only woman he needs to try stopping or minimizing it.

121. After a man gets caught cheating, why does he act like it's not a big deal, but once a woman gets caught, he acts like it's the end of the world?

When a man cheats, it's normally with a woman he has no true feelings for, meaning it's just a fling, but when a woman cheats, she has all types of emotions involved, and may even care about the person she's cheated with. This notion is from a lot of men's points of view, and it causes them to feel slightly different about men cheating than women cheating, but it really comes down to men being selfish because there isn't a difference. Cheating is cheating no matter with whom, how, when, where, or why it's done.

THE MALE TIP: Remind him that it's a two-way street. Cheating is the same crime no matter who commits it.

122. Why doesn't he think cheating involves talking, texting, and flirting with other women?

Some men think those types of situations are minor or harmless compared to going on dates or having sex with another woman. They are simple, harmless, and friendly exchanges with no real intention to cheat, so some men don't think of it as cheating. I personally think they could pass as a form of cheating depending on how far the conversations and flirting go.

THE MALE TIP: Be attentive of the types of conversations he has with other women because it will help you determine if lines are being crossed. Also, if too much conversing and flirting are going on between him and another woman, let him know how you feel about it. Cheating can and sometimes does involve talking, texting, or flirting, depending on the context.

123. Why does he feel like he can cheat or do whatever he wants just because he has a lot of money?
He might think he's a man of power. Some wealthy men consider themselves to have power over others, so they think they can get away with and do a lot of things other people can't. To get more in depth, since the world today is so money hungry and power driven, a lot of us think that people of power and wealth can do what they want with less or without consequences and repercussions than others, as well as being able to date anyone they want. Therefore, a wealthy man may feel like he can do things like cheat knowing that a woman may still stick by his side simply because he has money to live the lifestyle a lot of people wish they can have. It's known to be a common story among wealthy men, especially celebrities.

THE MALE TIP: Don't allow a man to disrespect you just because he's wealthy. Demand respect.

23

Lies and Deceit

On some households and relationships, lies are an everyday affair, and men will give you several excuses why they lie. I know you agree that a lot of men lie about the silliest things, from where they were the night before to details about their past relationships, sexual encounters, and so on. Whatever the lie, they seem to have no problem telling it, sometimes without remorse. Some lies you hear are harmless, and some lies you hear can be very damaging, but no matter what, a man will always have an excuse as to why he did it.

124. Why does he still lie after I tell him I'd rather hear the truth no matter how bad the truth hurts?
No matter how much you tell a man you'd rather hear the truth, he's still going to feel the need to lie if it's about

something he thinks will hurt your feelings or cause problems in the relationship. Sometimes when people tell us to
tell the truth no matter how bad it might be, it's just a tactic
used to get an honest confession and could have more consequences, repercussions, and emotions involved than they say
it does. So if he still lies after you tell him you'd rather hear
the truth, he's probably thinking that the truth is too much
of a burden and may upset, disappoint, or hurt your feelings although you're telling him it's better that way. If that's
not the case, then he may be what's called a compulsive liar,
meaning he lies out of habit, and it's his normal and reflex-
ive way of responding to questions.

THE MALE TIP: Try to be as forgiving as possible when he does
tell the truth so that he'll feel comfortable doing it regularly. If he's just a compulsive liar, take him to counseling or
a mental-health professional.

125. Why does he lie about his past relationships?

He may not want you to know or doesn't want to have to give
details about who he has dated or slept with in the past. He
probably feels he's dated too many women in the past, or
he may want to avoid making you jealous, disappointed, or
disenchanted of him from some of the women he might describe, or he just doesn't want you to be too curious to the
point that you might begin to want to know every single detail about his past. The most common reason men lie about
it is because they want their partner to look at them in a
good light, but if his past is disappointing, it could give a
woman a different perspective of the type of man he might

be, whether marriage material or not. Although a person's past shouldn't have any effect on their relationship, sometimes it does.

THE MALE TIP: Try not to be too focused on or concerned about his past relationships. If it's something you feel like you need to know, be patient and allow him to feel comfortable about telling you so that he's truthful. Also, make those types of conversations welcoming, and do not judge his flaws or mistakes.

126. Why do men lie about where they've been all day?

Because the truth might upset you. Wherever he's been might be a place that he knows you don't like or care for him going. Or he's probably the private type and prefers you not knowing his every move and everywhere he decides to go.

THE MALE TIP: Let him enjoy his freedom of going places without questioning his every move because it can make him feel as if you don't trust him. If he lies about where he goes, then you might want to consider it and do some investigating because it might be a place that he shouldn't be going.

127. Why do men lie about their true feelings or motives toward women and the relationship?

Those men don't want you to know their true feelings or exact plans because they like to be in control or steps ahead of a woman. Or it could also be that they don't want to put themselves in a position to be hurt or taken advantage of.

Also, men know that a lot of women are nosey, so some lie because they prefer a bit of privacy of their true feelings and motives. Furthermore, I believe that most men may lie to get what they want out of a woman since the truth might not get it.

THE MALE TIP: Try letting him voluntarily tell you about his feelings or motives in regards to you or your relationship with him. Don't force it out of him because if he doesn't want you to know now, there's a good chance you won't hear the truth. To find out whether he's lying only to get what he wants out of you, focus on his actions more than on his words. If he says he loves you but doesn't do much to show it, be cautious about it.

128. Why do men lie to make themselves look better?

This isn't just a male issue. This is a people issue. Male or female, a lot of people lie to make themselves look better to make it seem they're keeping up with the Joneses or doing well in life although they may be struggling with common issues. This is also something men lie about to get what they want out of a woman because we all know that the better a man is physically, spiritually, and mentally, the more the woman will be attracted and more likely to give.

THE MALE TIP: Have evidence of whatever it is he might tell you. For example, what he does for a living, the place he resides at, what he's been up to, and so forth. Don't just believe anything you hear from a man.

24

Trust

Trust in a relationship is one of the most important things to have being that good relationships are built around it. A couple of known facts about trust are that it plays a major role in determining whether you have a healthy or unhealthy relationship, and it's something that's difficult to sustain and even more difficult to regain once it's lost. Trusting your partner abundantly can make for a healthy relationship, but lacking trust can be the cause of an unhealthy one, and in a lot of relationships, men are the ones who have the hardest time fully trusting their partner. In some instances, men and women will come into a relationship not trusting their partner without giving them a chance to be trusted, depending on the experiences they've had in past relationships, which we now refer to as "having trust issues." Although a woman may be the main cause of her man losing trust in her, there are many other instances where a man doesn't trust women simply because of his own insecurities.

129. Why doesn't he trust me at all?

Either you've given him a reason that caused him not to trust you or he's just not the trusting type. As mentioned previously, some men have major trust issues, which could be the case with your partner. If it's not, then you've probably given him a reason not to trust you. For example, you may have lied to him about certain things, he may have put his trust in you to do something and you let him down by not getting it done, and so forth. There can be plenty of other scenarios of why you may have lost his trust, but with men it's normally from something you or another woman from his past has done to him. It's rare for a man not to trust a woman simply because of stories from other people's experiences about things like women lying, cheating, and so forth.

THE MALE TIP: If he doesn't have trust issues because of someone else, ask him whether it was something you've done that caused him to lose trust in you. If his trust is something you'd like to regain, from now on make sure you do everything with honesty, loyalty, and integrity. Exceed his expectations and try not to disappoint, and you should slowly but surely gain his trust back.

130. Why doesn't he trust me with his money?

A lot of men don't trust women with their money. It may sound stereotypical, but a lot of women are known to have spending problems, going shopping, spending money on unnecessary things, and so forth, before making sure every bill is paid on time with the necessities and priorities handled first and with money left to save. This is an issue in many relationships, and to say it directly, he doesn't trust your spending habits or feel that you're responsible enough to handle his finances. If you don't manage your money well, a man will not trust you to handle his.

THE MALE TIP: Try not to be concerned about this issue. Let him trust you with his finances when he's ready. Give him time to feel secure and comfortable about it. If it's something that you need to be involved in, show him that you can handle your own finances safely, securely, and correctly, and this should allow him to feel positive about trusting you with his.

131. Why doesn't he trust me coming home during wee hours?

A lot of men think there's nothing but trouble as well as more chances of infidelity happening during those hours, and there may have been things that he's experienced or witnessed in the past that make him feel that way. For example, criminal activities, recreational drug use, one-night stands, cheating, and other negative happenings all seem to happen more often during the late night and early morning hours.

Because of this, a lot of men are either uncomfortable with or don't trust their partner at all hanging out during those hours. But although he may have legitimate reasons why he doesn't trust it, I'd say it's more of an insecurity issue.

THE MALE TIP: Be responsible if you decide to hang out during those hours. Also, try to respect your partner's wishes as much as possible if he doesn't feel comfortable with you hanging out that late. Remember it's not only about respecting your partner but also respecting your relationship.

132. Why doesn't he trust my male friends?

The possibility of what could happen between you and your male friends when you become hurt, vulnerable, or revengeful may make him uncomfortable. To be a bit more specific, sometimes a woman looks to fill a void in her life by using one of her male friends to do certain things she can't or doesn't do with her partner because he's not interested, and when she does, she may become vulnerable or too close with another man resulting in the possibility of them doing things they shouldn't be doing such as sleeping with each other, kissing, touching, and so forth—basically, taking the friendly relationship a little too far—and that is something some male friends prey upon. The whole thought of it makes a lot of men uncomfortable and possibly insecure. Therefore, it causes us to not trust women having male friends. Also, you wanting or needing a male friend could make him jealous if he feels that he should be the only male you need.

THE MALE TIP: If he doesn't trust you having male friends, consider getting rid of them, especially if it risks jeopardizing your relationship. If he allows you to have them, keep communication between them at a minimum as it will minimize assumptions, doubts, and questions that could cause altercations between you and him. Show that he can trust you to have male friends by being responsible and respectful around them.

133. Why doesn't he trust my single female friends?

This is because single female friends are known to look, flirt, date, or converse with other men, possibly persuading you to do the same when hanging out with them or just gossiping with them. He just doesn't trust that they won't try influencing you to do certain things you shouldn't be doing while in a relationship. We all know what type of effect hanging out with single friends can have on our actions, both for males and females.

THE MALE TIP: Be selective about where you choose to hang out with your single friends. Also, stay away from the things they involve you in that you shouldn't be doing such as having personal conversations with other guys—basically doing things only single ladies should be doing, as it will minimize arguments between you and your partner.

Part Five

BAD TASTES IN YOUR MOUTH: Questions and Answers about Your Past, Problems Surrounding Your Cell Phone, Your Baby's Father (If Any), The Malarkey, and Him Catching Feelings

25

Your Past

I'm sure you know that some men will make your past very relevant in your current relationship by constantly trying to discuss it and asking questions about it. Common questions such as who you've dated, the number of guys you've slept with, and the type of things you've done are sometimes asked throughout your current relationship, which I've heard from other women is very annoying and frustrating at times. The funny thing is that a man will ask and want to know every single detail about some of your past although he doesn't know how to handle the answer or even believe what you're saying. I'm sure this is something many women get tired of because the things a woman has done in the past should not be brought into her future relationships;

however, a ton of women don't understand why it's so important for some of us to know about our woman's past.

134. Why does he want to know specific details about my past and past relationships?

He wants to make sure he feels comfortable with your past and the type of person you may have been, if different from now. He may also be the type of guy who compares your current relationship to your previous relationships to make sure he's considered one of your better relationships or one of your better sexual partners. The reasoning for most men wanting to know about their woman's past all falls under the fact that they want to make sure they're comfortable with the type of woman she was and is and that she is the type that they can bring home to mom and speak proudly about to their friends—a woman they're happy with spending the rest of their lives with.

THE MALE TIP: Try to discuss your past as openly and honestly as possible. Allow him to understand you by answering his questions as thoroughly as possible. Understand that avoiding the questions might cause concern or frustration depending on how important it is for him to know about your past.

135. What makes him bring up my past every so often?

Maybe he feels you didn't provide all the details yet, it's his way of making sure you've told him the truth the first time, there's something new that he wants to know every so often, or it's about something that bothers or agitates him, which causes him to bring it up to get it off his chest or relieve it from his mind.

THE MALE TIP: Continue to openly and honestly discuss the things he wants to know. If you're not comfortable with him constantly bringing it up, say that to him. Understand that it may or may not do any justice, but it's worth a try because when a man wants to know something, he will try his best to find out. You could even go as far as reassuring him that your current relationship with him is the only one that matters.

136. What makes him disappointed with something I did in my past?

It's probably toward something he thought you'd never do. When a man thinks highly of his woman or thinks she'd never do such a thing, it can disappoint him once he hears otherwise. Sort of like when a parent hears that his or her child has done something bad that he or she never thought the child would do—it can be highly disappointing.

THE MALE TIP: Again, reassure or comfort him in a way that allows him to feel unconcerned about anything that has disappointed him about your past.

137. Why does he want to know how many guys I've slept with?

To say it delicately, he wants to make sure you weren't too promiscuous having slept with a ton of guys. He might also want to know to see if he's special or important or just another guy on the list, or he might want to make sure you're a woman with morals, dignity and self-respect, and knowing how many guys you've slept with can give him an idea of that. Some men just prefer to be in a relationship with a woman who hasn't had a ton of sex partners.

THE MALE TIP: Answer the question truthfully. If it's an answer that you're somewhat ashamed of or regret, communicate that to him, and remind him that the guys you've slept with really shouldn't have to be discussed, and they shouldn't be a concern.

138. Why does he get mad when I voluntarily talk about my past relationships?

He doesn't care to hear it. If a man doesn't ask, most of the time that means he doesn't want to know, and it can upset him if your past is disappointing. For example, if you begin talking about the different things you've done with different guys, the number and type of guys you've slept with, and so forth, and your responses are disappointing to him, it could turn him off or make him upset, especially if he thought differently of you and didn't expect your past to be that way. Although the past should be left in the past, some men just can't stand to hear about their woman's old romances.

THE MALE TIP: Do not bring up your past relationships unless you know for a fact it's something he wants to talk about. If you ever decide to discuss it voluntarily, remind him that it means nothing and that it does not affect anything in the present. Also, when discussing it, don't make him feel like you're reminiscing about good times in past relationships with other men because it might make him a bit jealous.

139. Why does he hate that I refuse to answer his questions about my past relationships?

For some men, refusing to talk about it could cause them to feel concerned. It could cause him to feel like you're hiding something, as if it's something that you know will make him think lesser of you or the relationship. No man wants to be fully in the dark about his woman's history, so refusing to talk about something he asks you about can make him feel that way. He might also get angry if he's passionate about knowing, but you don't tell.

THE MALE TIP: Try to talk about it with an open mind without refusal. Do not make him feel like he's in the dark about knowing and understanding your past and who you are. Sometimes it's more comforting for a man to know, especially if he asks.

26

Cell-Phone Issues

We all know how secretive a man and his cell phone can be. Sometimes he tends to act as if it's a safe-deposit box, never wanting anyone, especially his woman, to gain access to it. Some men even act like a lunatic as soon as their woman tries or gets hold of it, but what men don't seem to realize is that it can—and a lot of times will—cause a woman to have insecurities about having a trustworthy and faithful relationship. It's very questionable why they act in such secretive ways regarding their phone, but it might be because they feel that they should be trusted or because they really are hiding something.

140. Why does he always have his phone facedown around me?

Some say it's just a habit, but doesn't there have to be reason for having such a habit? Normally, yes, and the only logical answer would be that he doesn't like how his phone lights up the whole room and catches everyone's attention, so he turns it upside down, or perhaps he doesn't want you to see who and if someone's calling because it might cause a problem depending on who the caller is. It could be another woman calling, one of his guy friends you don't like, or someone who gives you a bad taste in your mouth that he communicates with. Whatever reason he gives, it's tough trying to determine if it's true or untrue.

THE MALE TIP: First try trusting that he does it harmlessly, maybe as just a habit, or maybe he enjoys a little privacy. Try not to let it bother you, but if it does, address it, and ask him why he does it—maybe you'll get an honest answer. If you believe that he does it because he's cheating or has other women calling, do whatever you can to find out the truth.

141. Why does he take his cell phone everywhere he goes in the house?

Either he's addicted to his phone, and this could be a real addiction, or he doesn't want you to get hold of it. If he's addicted to it, that just means he likes to use it wherever he goes and has a hard time leaving it alone. If he does it so you won't get hold of it, then there are probably some things inside it that he considers private or possibly damaging to the relationship. A lot of people, male and female, don't like anyone sneaking through their phones, so some of them will always take their phones with them to prevent that from happening.

THE MALE TIP: If him taking his phone everywhere in the house makes you feel any type of way, express it to him. Don't allow it to bother you, and do speak up about it because it could eventually cause you to think there's some infidelity going on or to feel that you aren't trusted or worthy enough to be around his phone.

142. Why doesn't he change his number or delete his ex-girlfriend's contact when I ask him to?

He may not want to change it because he might have a lot of history with that number or may have had it for a long time and doesn't want to go through the hassle of having to notify friends, colleagues, and businesses of his new number. There could also be people whom he doesn't want to get rid of or people he wants to continue to converse with such as an ex-girlfriend or close lady friend. Make note that whenever a man refuses to delete any of his past girlfriends out of his phone, it normally means he wants to make sure he has access to them in case something happens within the current relationship that allows him to communicate with her.

THE MALE TIP: Either bear with him when it comes to having him change his number or deleting ex-girlfriends' contacts, or demand him to get it done ASAP considering that it would be more beneficial for your current relationship.

143. Why does he keep a passcode on his phone and doesn't want or let me go through it?
In relationships, men and women keep passcodes on their phones because they feel that it's their own personal device, not something everyone should have access to, for privacy reasons. There may be embarrassing, unexpected, damaging, disappointing, and for-his-eyes-only types of things on his phone that he doesn't want you to see—possibly cheating acts or simple harmless things. Also, some men only keep a passcode on their phone to keep their private information—things like accounts, finances, and important contacts safe and secure in case their phone gets lost or stolen.

THE MALE TIP: Accept the fact that some men enjoy privacy for their cell phones. If it's a healthy and trusting relationship, there shouldn't be any reason why you need to go through his phone, and there also shouldn't be any reason why he never lets you. If he acts extremely private about it, then you may need to be cautious because he might not be as trusting as you think.

144. Why is his phone always on silent when around me, especially at night?
Either he doesn't like getting phone calls at night waking him up, or he's getting unacceptable phone calls from someone who could damage the relationship, such as another woman.

We all know a phone being on silent means that a person is trying to avoid the phone call or avoid hearing it ring so that the partner won't notice who's calling, and these are just about the only two reasons why a man will put his phone on silent at home and at night. It doesn't mean they're up to no good, although a lot of women assume they are. Some men will even tell you they do it because they don't want anyone interrupting their quality time with their partner, which can be true.

THE MALE TIP: If his phone being on silent makes you uncomfortable, let him know how you feel and what you think about it. If he says he does it to avoid interruption, trust that he's telling the truth. Don't assume the worst until you have proof of the worst because assuming can possibly hurt your relationship.

145. Why does he get mad or suspicious when my phone rings late at night?

He might think it's another guy calling, or he's the type of guy who thinks there's nothing that important that anyone could need to talk with you about at that time of night. Since we know that a man will call a woman any time of night only for certain things, we get suspicious when a woman gets a call during that time. It's almost like a natural reaction, but it's safe to say that it's vice versa with women because some women have that same reaction when a man's phone rings late at night. It's all assumptions though, so he's getting mad or suspicious because he's assuming it's another guy calling.

THE MALE TIP: Prove to him that there's nothing to worry about when your phone rings late at night. Maybe even show him who's calling to prevent suspicion. Also, be respectful to him when conversing with someone late at night by speaking with a low tone and keeping the conversation short.

27

Your Child's Father ("Baby Daddy")

For men, dealing with another child's father can be very difficult, sometimes even frustrating. There may be moments where both males don't get along with each other, moments where they have their disagreements, and moments where they clash for certain reasons involving the child. Some women understand the reasons why these types of feuds occur between their partner and the child's father, but some women think they're highly unnecessary. Not only is it unnecessary at times, but it can also cause a great deal of stress and make for an unhealthy relationship if it isn't handled properly by either party, which is why it should always be treated delicately and carefully, especially by a woman.

WHY MEN THIS, WHY MEN THAT?

If the actions between you and your child's father as far as decisions, communication, agreements, and so forth pertaining to your child aren't accepted by your current partner, it can be the reason for him acting in such ways that are questioned below. For example, too many unnecessary conversations between you and your child's father can cause him to feel uncomfortable about you conversing with him at all, or mentioning him too freely and too often could cause him to feel as if you still have some sort of close relationship with him outside of the responsibilities of your child. Those types of things will cause a man to react in certain ways toward you or the child's father that many women question or may not understand.

146. Why doesn't he feel comfortable with me talking to my child's father or meeting him whenever I go to pick up my kid?

He may not trust the fact that you're only going to do that, meaning he might feel that you guys are out doing other things besides picking your child up. When it comes to conversing with your child's father, he may feel uncomfortable about it if he thinks it's possible for you or him to gain feelings back for each other because of it, and we all know how that can make for an unfaithful situation. All of it is pretty much caused by trust issues or from something that you've done in the past that caused him to feel uncomfortable about it.

THE MALE TIP: Prove to him that there's nothing else happening between you and your child's father besides the handling of your kid. Keep the conversations with your child's father at a minimum. You could even try bringing your partner along when meeting to pick up your child, and this might make your partner feel more comfortable. If he doesn't want you conversing or meeting with your child's father at all, try your best to find ways to do so. Making your partner comfortable about these situations can make for a better relationship between both of you.

147. Why doesn't he feel comfortable talking to my child's father?

It could be him not liking the fact that you have a kid by another guy, let alone having to communicate with him, or if your child's father has been disrespectful toward you or him, it can cause him to not want to deal with conversing with him. Or he's just the type of guy who doesn't like communicating with men you've had relations with.

THE MALE TIP: Don't force him into conversing with your child's father. Be patient because he will when he's ready. If he feels that he never needs to discuss anything with him, let him do that unless it's truly a necessity.

148. Why would he rather not get along with my child's father?

Since dealing with another child's father is known to have its differences or issues, he probably prefers avoiding the possibility of it, and not getting along with him is his way of doing so. He could also not want to get along with him if he's been disrespected by him or if your child's father has been disrespectful to you in any way. Some men are sensitive to the whole dealing with a child's father situation so any small thing could cause them to not want to get along with a woman's baby's father.

THE MALE TIP: Do not force them to get along with each other, and do your best to keep them from having issues with each other because those kinds of issues can cause you to conflict with your current partner or add tension to your relationship.

149. Why does he constantly mention my child's father?
He could be jealous of him or despise him for whatever reason; maybe it's the fact that you have a child with someone else or that you must deal with him because of the child. Things such as that can cause him to constantly discuss or mention your child's father because the whole situation bothers him, and we all know that when something like that bothers someone, he or she wants to talk about it or get it off the chest.

THE MALE TIP: Make him feel comfortable about whatever it is that may be bothering him by discussing it calmly and with honesty. You could also try asking him why he mentions him so much, although he may not give you an honest answer being that a man doesn't want to tell the woman he loves that he doesn't like the fact that she has a kid by another guy, if that's the reason. Involve him in the decisions you and the child's father must make regarding the child so that he won't feel like another man has more say-so than he does when it comes to your child and your household. Focus on making him as comfortable as possible about being a stepdad.

150. Why does he not like when my child's father makes certain decisions regarding my child?

He probably feels like your child's father is controlling things that he shouldn't be, or it makes him feel like the household is being run by him in a way. When men are in relationships, they aren't fond of another man making decisions that involve their partner or family especially if it's about a child who lives in their household. It may be complicated to explain and maybe only understood by men, but to say it in simpler terms, a lot of men consider themselves the head of the household, and letting another man make decisions regarding their family goes against that perception. It's also possible that he just doesn't like your child's father.

THE MALE TIP: Don't allow your child's father to have full control over such decisions because it could cause friction between you and your current partner. Discuss everything with your current partner before letting your child's father make any final decisions.

151. Can he ever get along with my child's father?

Yes and no. It depends on the circumstances and whether he's the forgiving type. If the reason he doesn't get along with him is personal enough that he holds a grudge against him, then I wouldn't expect him to get along with him anytime soon. However, if the reason is minor, then not getting along with each other could just be temporary. Hopefully, not much damage was done.

THE MALE TIP: Find out why he doesn't get along with him, and try to fix it as best as you can. If it's something you have no control over, just be patient and give him time. It's a touchy subject because sometimes it's best not to get involved; let them handle it between themselves.

28

The Malarkey

This topic addresses some of the most random and unusual questions asked by women today. Malarkey is defined as meaningless talk and nonsense that people give, and this is an issue a lot of women experience since men have the tendency to speak a bunch of it habitually. Although it may seem natural among both men and women, women seem to be more on the receiving end because men dish it out the most. Common instances such as us bullcrapping about when we'll be ready for marriage or about us liking our woman's family although we don't are both instances that a lot of women are familiar with since they're common stories told by a lot of us. There's plenty more instances that you and others may have heard about or experienced, but the most familiar are explained in this section.

152. Why does he bullcrap me about him going to the gym to get a better body, but he actually doesn't go?

If a man isn't truthful about going to the gym, it's probably a cover up to have free time to go and do something else. It's one of the easiest and most believable excuses a man can use. If he doesn't do it for the free time for doing something else, he does it to impress you by making you believe he's being proactive and concerned about his health because some women are proud of and aroused by a man who's concerned about his health and physique.

THE MALE TIP: Go to the gym with him if you want to make sure that's where he's going. You could even go as far as trying to pay attention to his training results because that might help you see if he's in the gym as much as he says he is.

153. Why does he bullcrap my family acting like he likes them when he doesn't?

A lot of men feel like they need to show a liking toward their woman's family because of how important and beneficial it can be to have a positive relationship with her family. It also helps to get the family's approval to continue to date and can make the relationship easier or less stressful because of all the issues not liking a woman's family can bring, especially if she's family oriented. It's just the respectful thing to do.

THE MALE TIP: Tell him to be truthful if it bothers you. But no matter what, treat the situation with maturity and sensitivity.

There should be a reason why he doesn't like them, so respect his reasoning. Not everyone will like or get along with each other. If it's a situation where you want him to like them, discuss it and help him work toward it. If he's too stubborn to do so, you may just need to accept it.

154. Why does he bullcrap his kids about spending time with them?

Either he isn't good with time management, meaning he tries to spend time with them but ends up doing other things that take up his day, or he doesn't care or make it a priority to spend time with them. Sometimes men get so busy with their schedule that they forget that they've told their kids they were going to spend time with them, on top of them forgetting that it should be a priority. Sad to say, but some men just tell their kids what they want to hear and have no intentions of spending time with them.

THE MALE TIP: Converse with him about making it a priority to spend time with his kids no matter how busy his schedule gets. Tell him not to mention spending time with them if he isn't going to because it will disappoint the children.

155. Why does he bullcrap me by telling me that my sex isn't good when he knows it is?

He probably doesn't want to fill your head up and allow you to become overly proud or conceited because some women are known to use such things to their advantage and act as if they are above all after they find out their sex is amazing. If that isn't the case, he probably just does it to joke around and get a laugh or response out of you.

THE MALE TIP: Tell him to be honest, but don't act conceited or boastful after he tells you. Other than that, just ignore it and continue having great sex.

156. Why does he bullcrap me about when we're getting married?

There could be several reasons why he does this. It could be that he's in fear of the whole marriage thing, he may not be 100 percent sure about marrying you, he may not feel the need to get married especially if things are going good and he doesn't want that to change, or he does it if you've given him that famous ultimatum a lot of women give, which is telling him that if he doesn't marry you within a few years, you want to move on elsewhere. Remember that some men don't feel the same as most women about marriage as far as thinking of it as a necessity or significant achievement, so men don't focus on it as much as a lot of women do.

THE MALE TIP: Ask him how he feels and what he thinks about marriage. Don't rush him into it—just be patient. He'll marry you when the time is right. If you do sort of rush him into it, don't give him any reasons to have negative thoughts about it.

29

Catching Feelings

Some men love expressing their feelings in their relationship while some others don't. Some gain feelings too fast, and some don't seem to gain them quick enough, but no matter how men express their feelings, would you agree that they seem to do it much differently and less than women? Although that may be true, all men need to understand how important it is to express their feelings regularly whether they like to or not because it can be beneficial to their relationship.

According to certain women, what's understood is that if a man doesn't catch and express his feelings enough, it can cause a woman to doubt him having the type of feelings he'll say he has for her or if he has any at all. However, what's not understood by some women is that just because a man doesn't express his feelings toward his woman, it doesn't mean that he doesn't love her. Some men don't like to catch feelings because they prefer to keep up a brick wall, mainly to avoid disappointment, and then there's the men who catch feelings quite easily. People have their reasoning why they do, why they don't, why they decide to wait, why they don't express them too much, why they hate it when their partner doesn't express them, and so forth. It's all just different strokes for different folks.

157. Why did he catch feelings so fast?

This just means you've given him, shown him, or told him something about yourself that he likes, is interested in, or turned on by. When a man is turned on by certain things, such as a woman's actions, interests, or presence, he might develop some type of feelings for her no matter whether he's known her for a short or long time. He could also lust for you so much that it caused him to catch feelings out of nowhere.

THE MALE TIP: Find out what you did that interested him and caused him to feel this way. If you have a problem with him moving too fast, express that to him, and ask for a bit of space, so the relationship won't feel rushed. Maybe cut back on seeing him or conversing with him if it's been too much.

158. Why does he act allergic to catching feelings?

He could be the type who thinks he's too manly to catch feelings, meaning he might feel as if it's too sensitive for his personality. Some men don't like to show certain emotions such as crying or being depressed because they feel that those types of emotions shouldn't be displayed by men. If that's not the case, then something may have happened to him in the past with a previous relationship or incident where he was disappointed or embarrassed after expressing certain feelings. He may not like to express those feelings anymore to avoid the same disappointment.

THE MALE TIP: Ask him if there was anything that happened to him in the past that may have caused him to feel this way about catching or expressing feelings. If it's something that bothers you, tell him how you feel about it. No man should act allergic to catching feelings, unless he's just careless about his relationship.

159. Why did he tell me right away that he doesn't catch feelings?

Either he doesn't want you to get the wrong idea not understanding what his intentions are for the relationship or he doesn't want you to expect anything more than what he plans to give. Men know that when a woman starts dating, she normally has hopes, plans, and expectations to be in a long-lasting relationship, so for a woman to not expect such things, a man might tell her in the beginning of the relationship that he doesn't catch feelings or doesn't want to. A man will also use this tactic to make sure a woman understands that he might not want to go as far in the relationship as she may want. It's mainly said to avoid certain things, but hopefully he's not the type who just has a cold heart and honestly doesn't catch feelings because there are men out there like that.

THE MALE TIP: Listen and take note when a man tells you he doesn't catch feelings, and act accordingly.

160. Why did he start acting different and seem disappointed after I told him I'm not going to catch feelings?

This normally happens if a man has hopes and plans for something more than just being close friends or acquaintances with you. When you tell a man something such as you're not interested or you won't catch feelings, it can cause him to think you're hinting at the fact that you're not looking for anything more than just a friend, which will cause him to back off or feel disappointed if he had other intentions.

THE MALE TIP: If you're not looking for anything more than just a friend, continue to be honest, and inform him beforehand so that he won't get any other ideas and to avoid disappointment. If you're looking for more than a friend, tell him what you mean by saying you're not going to catch feelings so he doesn't have to guess.

161. Why did he act like he didn't catch feelings until after the sex?

Although a lot of you might say "This is your typical man," catching feelings after sex is somewhat common and happens for several reasons with men. It happens with some men because the sex might have made them feel closer than they've ever been to that woman causing their feelings to get deeper. Some men prefer to wait after intercourse to be fully involved with a woman to make sure they connect well on a physical, emotional, and sexual level. Also, believe it or not, a man might use the act as a tactic to have intercourse sooner than expected especially if the woman is interested in him. It might be rare, but it happens.

THE MALE TIP: Make sure he has feelings for you before the intercourse. There's nothing more genuine and authentic than a relationship with a man who didn't need intercourse to have or show feelings for you.

Part Six

FAMILY MATTERS: Questions and Answers about Stress, Responsibilities, Employment, Finances, Marriage, and Children

30

Stress

The stress being discussed in this chapter is defined as a state of mental or emotional strain or tension resulting from adverse or very demanding circumstances. In simpler terms, it's strong feelings of worry or anxiety. These days in relationships, stress resulting from one another's actions happens as often as eating breakfast, lunch, and dinner. Some would even agree that it's inescapable, not only in relationships but in everyday life also. One reason is that the smallest, simplest events or conditions can trigger stress. Although men and women have the same or similar types of stressors, I'd say we handle or react differently to it. For example, a woman might cry or prefer to talk about it with friends, family, and so forth to relieve it, while a lot of males prefer to engage in some type of activity such as exercising,

golfing, or others. Aside from us handling it differently, a lot of times we act biased toward who's to blame for the reason we're stressed, which is one reason why it's a constant issue that women question and are concerned about in their relationship because the blame is always aimed toward them.

162. Why does he take all his stress out on me and our relationship?

It's possible that he thinks the relationship is the reason he's stressed. If he's unhappy or disappointed about certain things within the relationship and believes you're the cause of it, then taking his stress out on you may be his way of expressing it. Or he's just acting like a lot of other human beings by taking his frustrations out on the closest known person available to him, which is you. Sometimes a man's partner is the easiest person to take his stress out on. He could also do it in a way to control you, by showing his anger and making you fear him to get you to do what he wants. It's sad but sometimes true.

THE MALE TIP: Try not to take it personal, and tell him how it makes you feel. If he does it excessively, he may need to seek counseling because it could be an issue that needs therapeutic attention. If nothing works, consider leaving the relationship.

163. Why does he tell me I'm the reason he's always stressed?

Either it's his way of taking his stress out on you or you really are the reason he's stressed. Again, there may be certain things you do or say that cause him to feel that way. For example, if you say things that constantly agitate or frustrate him or if you do things that constantly disappoint or annoy him, more than likely it will make him feel like you're the reason for his stress. Also, it's possible that he says it if he's to the point where even the smallest sight of you annoys him.

THE MALE TIP: Try to avoid things that might agitate, frustrate, or disappoint him. Also, find ways to turn his stress into positivity so that he can view you as a helpmate, not a culprit.

164. Why does it seem like he stresses me out on purpose?
When a man stresses you out on purpose, it means either he enjoys your reaction, meaning it's entertainment for him, or he's upset or bothered by you and does it to get revenge.

THE MALE TIP: There's no sure way to know if he's doing it purposely unless he tells you, but if you think he is, try addressing it to him. Tell him everything, from what you think about it to how it makes you feel and what type of damage it does.

165. Why does he get so stressed over disagreements?
Either he's the type of man who hates to be wrong or he hates when your thoughts, opinions, or interests don't coincide with his. When things happen such as you not finding a way to agree, it can cause you to clash, which causes some men to become angered and stressed. Although you might think that

disagreeing isn't that serious and is nothing to be stressed about, he on the other hand might feel differently.

THE MALE TIP: Sometimes you should agree to disagree, and remind him that disagreeing doesn't mean he's wrong or that he'll be looked at any different or less. Also, find ways to allow peace and calmness during times of stress because it can help eliminate negativity.

31

Responsibilities and Priorities

It's probably safe to say that women are more responsible than men in terms of handling and prioritizing things in their relationships. It might even be the reason they seem to end up having more responsibilities to deal with than their partners, but no matter who's responsible for what, it can be an issue that causes conflict or concern if they aren't handled correctly. But not only are responsibilities sometimes a cause for concern, the managing of priorities can be as well. For example, common instances women have dealt with is a man putting his friends before her and the relationship, forgetting to pay one of the bills on time, or not buying the things needed before buying the things wanted. Besides these instances, there are plenty more that women have to deal with, but the moral of the story is that dealing with a man and the reasons why he isn't prioritizing correctly the way a man should or the reasons he's not responsible always causes concern and can be extremely hard to deal with.

166. Why doesn't he take care of his responsibilities in the relationship before anything else?

First off, not every man and woman have the same outlook on what's considered a responsibility in their relationship, so the type of things that you think and feel are responsibilities may not be the same as what he thinks. Second, his priorities may not be in order, meaning his focus isn't on what should be primarily important in a relationship. Third, he may just be incompetent, not having the knowledge, interests, or skill in recognizing and making sure the responsibilities in the relationship are handled before anything else.

THE MALE TIP: Discuss what both of you consider to be responsibilities in your relationship. Help each other get the job done. Don't take it personally if he has a habit of forgetting or not caring; just find ways to deal with the type of person he is. Also, address whatever issue you have, so he'll know what to work toward.

167. Why does it seem like it's so hard for him to be a responsible man?

Again, you guys might not consider or have the same views on what responsibilities are, so it's possible that he thinks he's responsible while you don't. It's also possible that he's arrogant, does what he wants, and is careless of what you think or say about whether he's responsible or not. If none of these pertain to him, then he's just a man who doesn't know how to be responsible, or he is, but you expect too much from him, which might make you think that he's not.

THE MALE TIP: In a respectable manner, express how you feel about thinking he's not responsible, but understand he might get offended. If he doesn't understand, try explaining to him in detail what you think a responsible man consists of. If he does understand but acts uninterested, then you pretty much have three options: accept it, continue to pressure him into becoming responsible, or leave the relationship.

168. Why does he act like our relationship isn't a priority?
To him it may not be. He might think that a relationship is a normal aspect of life, so he doesn't look at it as anything special or of great importance, and men with that type of mind-set sometimes think that a relationship is nothing to prioritize. If he does think that the relationship is a priority but acts the opposite, he doesn't realize he's acting that way; he's so consumed with other things in his life that he puts the relationship on the backburner, or he purposely acts that way for a reason.

THE MALE TIP: Mention it and give him time to change it. If he thinks relationships aren't a priority, and you're bothered by his way of thinking, express yourself to him, but at the same time, understand and realize that it's okay for people to have their own opinions. If his way of thinking affects the nature of the relationship in a negative way, then you may need to suggest he seek counseling for it or figure out ways to deal with it.

169. Why does he have to give me the money to pay the bills as if he isn't responsible enough to do so?

This may not be a responsibility issue. Some men just prefer to give their woman the money to pay the bills because it's a traditional practice to leave the woman in charge of handling it, especially if he's the one providing all the funds to do so. He probably witnessed his parents or elders handling the bills that way, and that mind-set was passed down to him. If he truly does need you to make sure the bills are paid on time, then he probably doesn't think he's responsible enough to do it himself without forgetting, or he doesn't want to be bothered by having to add another responsibility to his life, so he passes it on to you. It's always easier to just give someone the money and let him or her deal with the rest.

THE MALE TIP: If it doesn't bother you, continue to keep the responsibility of paying bills on time. However, if it does, try mixing it up a little bit by having him handle it here and there. You could even try handling them together.

32

Employment

en's thoughts about women being employed or unemployed in relationships are probably one of the most opinionated topics ever discussed. Aside from that, many different questions from women surround the topic. For more than a century, women's rights to work were deemed an issue and were discussed among men around the entire world, but nowadays the discussions that seem to matter most are related to a couple deciding how they will handle employment: Will they both work full-time? Will the woman be a stay-at-home mom? What type of jobs will she work? and so forth. Some men prefer their woman to be employed while some prefer them to be unemployed, and a lot of women don't really understand the reasoning behind men's decisions about it. After you've read this section you'll have a better understanding of why men prefer women to be both employed and unemployed, plus you'll get the answers to other common related questions.

170. Why does it matter to him what I do for a living?
If working a job that makes good money matter to him, then he's probably more comfortable being in a relationship that has financial security, not having to stress about financial situations, or he may feel the need to have a partner who has a high social status, which is a rank or position within society that he can feel or brag confidently about to whomever such as friends or family. He could also be attracted to the fact that you have an excellent occupation. The unfortunate reason why your occupation might matter is if he's the type of guy who hates for a woman whom he's in a relationship with to make more money than him. That matters to some men and can be upsetting.

THE MALE TIP: All you can really do is understand and respect how he feels and possibly aim for an occupation that he'll feel happy about, but I wouldn't recommend that unless you feel it's best for you and your family as well. Do not choose a career based on someone else's decision—do what makes you happy.

171. Why isn't he motivated to get a better job for us?
He's probably not the type who's career driven, or he's so comfortable with whatever position he's in now that he doesn't feel the need to become motivated and strive for anything greater. This truly is a common issue among men, so

you're not alone, but the fact of the matter is that there are two types of men in the world—those who strive for greatness and those who prefer comfort and staying stagnant, so recognize which type you're dating.

THE MALE TIP: Try becoming his motivation, and push him to do better. If that doesn't help, you may need to reconsider whom you're dating.

172. Why doesn't he like me working tough labor jobs?
When a man doesn't like for a woman to work tough labor jobs, it normally is because he believes that those types of jobs are a man's job. Think of it like him being considerate rather than doubting your abilities. That type of mind-set either comes from how he was raised or the understanding of the traditional concept of how a man should work doing the hard labor and the woman should take care of the household. Some men or women would think of it as him being a gentleman by not liking or allowing you to work tough labor jobs while some would think he's being sexist. Understand that there's always a possibility that it could be a sexist issue, but it's mainly just a man trying to be a man by being as considerate as possible to his partner and allowing the tough jobs to be his responsibility, not his woman's.

THE MALE TIP: Go ahead and leave the hard labor jobs to him, but if you truly feel that working one yourself is necessary or satisfying, then discuss it with him. Also, converse with him about it to get a better understanding about why he doesn't like you working those types of jobs; that way you can make an honest decision about working them and minimize any altercation it might cause.

173. Why doesn't he act 100 percent supportive of me going back to school to get a better job?
This just means he has his own opinions about it. He might feel that it's not a good time for you to go back to school; he might feel like you could be doing more productive types of things that are in the now instead of the patient school route, and he might also feel like if you attend school, it might change a lot of things in both his life and yours considering it would be an addition to your schedule, altering it in ways that might affect his. He probably just has so many thoughts and opinions toward the matter that it causes him to think that going to school isn't the best decision for you now, although it may be in the long run.

THE MALE TIP: Remind him that he needs to be supportive of your decisions, especially a decision so important that could affect both of you guys' future if you plan on being in a long-term relationship together.

174. Why does he prefer I stay at home instead of getting a job?
This normally means that he's the type of guy who prefers to pay the bills and be the financial provider for everything while you handle the rest or most of the other household and family chores, like the role of the housewife or stay-at-home

mom. Another possibility is that he might think it's more beneficial and cost saving if you stay unemployed. Some families benefit by getting some type of government assistance for their child if the household doesn't make enough income, which is done by only one person showing income. Believe it or not, it pays more to get financial assistance instead of both parents working having to pay for things like daycare. Some take advantage of the system, but it's not the right thing to do.

THE MALE TIP: Do what's best for you depending on what you think is more important: satisfying his preference, doing what makes you happy, or doing what's best for your family. It should be your decision to make.

175. Why does he want me to get a job instead of staying home?

He might think you'd have too much time on your hands and get bored if you stayed unemployed. He might also want you to work because having that second income would be more helpful than one. Or he doesn't think that there's a legitimate or beneficial reason for you to not have a job.

THE MALE TIP: Converse with him about it, and try to come up with an agreement based on what's best for the relationship or family.

33

Finances

Relationships and finances almost go hand in hand. Some couples even have relationships based on financial gain. Although every couple handles their finances differently, the same types of problems still exist. For example, arguments over common monetary issues such as poor spending habits, who pays for what pertaining to bills and outings, and keeping incomes private. Whether you're involved in a good relationship or not, financial issues and disagreements can always make for a depressing or confrontational relationship. Some couples literally sit down and discuss finances together in order to keep a stable relationship and a solid understanding of how money will be spent and handled. That type of approach should be recommended to most couples to avoid as many financial issues as possible, unless it's a couple that gets by just fine without having to do so. Back in the day, finances were more of a man's responsibility, but it seems like times are changing, and it's becoming more of an equal responsibility. A lot of older couples follow the same tradition of men taking care of the family financially and paying for things such as dates and outings. Although it's followed by some younger couples as well, it's becoming not so common and popular as it was in the past. Finances are a sensitive topic, and some couples don't even like discussing their financial status, but no matter what the issue is financially within relationships, a lot of them are common issues almost every couple goes through.

176. Why does he care about making more money than me?
It's mainly a pride issue for a lot of men. He might have the mind-set of being the breadwinner and provider of the family, so it's pretty much instilled in him to care about how much money you make. Although he can still be the main provider regardless of how much you make, it can take that breadwinner or provider title away from him mentally if you bring home more money than he does. It could also cause him to feel as if he has failed at being the man he should or was supposed to be. There are other intricate reasons why a man might care to make more money than his woman does, but all of them are mainly a result of having too much pride.

THE MALE TIP: If you make more than him, allow him to still be the man who he thinks he is or should be. Also, avoid mentioning the fact that you make more because it could cause conflict or tension between both of you depending on how deeply he feels about it. Always be cordial when it comes to discussing you and your partner's finances.

177. Why doesn't he like me to pay for things like dates, outings, and so forth?

On a positive note, he may just feel like it's a man's job to pay for everything. It's also sometimes a man's way of being a gentleman, being considerate, and showing his manners. On a negative note, some men use it as a ploy to get something in return or to make a woman feel in debt toward them, but that's not normally the case in most relationships. In most relationships, it's because of a man's positive attributes such as his manners, obligations, and expectations.

THE MALE TIP: Let him pay for the things that he expects to pay for. You could offer to pay every now and then out of generosity and to remind him that your relationship involves togetherness. Don't forget to show your appreciation from time to time; a simple "Thank you" can go a long way.

178. Why does a man feel like he can get away with anything if he brings in all the money?

Bringing in all the money in the household gives some men a feeling of control and causes them to think that they shouldn't have to suffer any consequences for any wrongdoings since you rely on them and don't pay for bills or anything else in the house. It kind of relates to the old saying "Money is power," and a lot of men truly do believe that they deserve the power of getting away with a lot of things especially if they're the only financial providers in their households. This issue is most common among athletes, celebrities, CEOs, and so forth.

THE MALE TIP: Remind him that that type of attitude is unacceptable and a relationship is still a partnership no matter how much money he makes. The relationship still must be respected.

179. Why does he keep his income private?

Some men don't want a woman involved with their income because she might feel like she has some say-so about how it's spent, how it's saved, and so forth, and to avoid arguments, disagreements, or confrontation about finances, he keeps it private. He could also be an extremely private person and doesn't like for people to know his business, or he could be embarrassed about it and prefer not to talk about it. A lot of men and women prefer to keep their incomes private because some people were just raised that way.

THE MALE TIP: Be understanding and respectful about his preferences. If it's not a big deal, continue to give him the freedom of keeping his income private. If it becomes a situation that is putting the relationship or household in jeopardy financially, discuss it with him, and suggest him to be more open about it so you can become better aware and involved with the handling and managing of finances together.

180. Why does it seem like he has an attitude whenever I ask him for money?

He might feel like you should be making your own money not needing to constantly ask for his, or he might think you're purchasing unnecessary items that are a waste of money. Some men don't want what's called a "gimme gimme girl," which is a woman who always has her hand out asking for favors or is constantly begging for things without doing any work herself to obtain it, and he might feel like you're that type of girl, which may not be a good feeling for him, causing him to get an attitude whenever you ask him for money. If you rarely ask him for money, but he still gets an attitude, he may just be selfish or cheap, and he might hate giving it to you.

THE MALE TIP: Don't make asking him for money a habit. Try only asking him when it's a necessity. If he gets an attitude no matter what, avoid asking as much as possible or altogether. Also, converse with him about it because every issue in relationships can be, or at least should be, resolved through simple discussion.

34

Marriage

To some, marriage is considered the greatest affirmation of love and symbol of unification between two individuals in a relationship. It's what a lot of women dream of—the almighty ring on the finger and everything else that comes along with it. Some women crave it, some women dream about it, and some are in constant search for it. One of the main reasons women want a marriage commitment is for a feeling of security. Although most women think highly of marriage, a lot of men don't seem as passionate as women are about it. Some men feel as if marriage is just another way to make their women happy or feel complete. However, don't be mistaken—a lot of men do agree that it's a very special moment and milestone in their lives.

It's just not as sought after by men as it is for women, and there are plenty of reasons why.

181. Why did he take so long to marry me, and what made him finally do it?

He wasn't sure if you or he were ready. A lot of things are involved when it comes to a man being ready. For example, a lot of men prefer to make sure they're at a great point in their life as far as their career, emotionally, or financially, or they need to make sure they're having positive thoughts about settling down and that you're the correct woman to marry. We all want to make sure we're making the right choice because marriage is a huge step in our lives, and some men don't agree with divorce or feel like it's an option, so marriage is final for some. As far as what made him want to, there could've been some type of wake-up call that made him feel like it was time. It could've been something you've done that triggered the decision, he may have realized that you're the best woman he's ever been with, or maybe the fact that you've been together so long and been through so much together made him decide you were the one. Let's just hope the only reason he married you wasn't because he felt like he was getting up in age and was so-called settling.

THE MALE TIP: Simply talk to him about it. If you're his wife or future wife, he shouldn't have any problems at all discussing it with you.

182. Why don't men want to get married as much as women do?

I wouldn't say this question pertains to all men but some of them, yes. Some men are fine being in a relationship without having to sign marriage paperwork. A lot of people feel like a lifelong relationship without marriage can work just as well as a happy marriage. Also, some men believe that marriage causes more drama or changes to the relationship because of more expectations being placed on the relationship. Rumor has it that things change once a man is married, which is one of the reasons why a lot of men are just fine staying in a relationship without getting married. And don't forget about the many laws that come into effect once you're married, like the fifty-fifty asset laws such as sharing houses, vehicles, pensions, and so forth, even though it may not have been paid for fifty-fifty or the issues you must deal with going through a divorce. There are just too many changes and things men rather not deal with that come with marriage, which is why some don't care to get married as much as women do or at all.

THE MALE TIP: If he doesn't want to get married or has unsure thoughts about it, remind him of all the positive aspects of marriage. If he's avoiding marriage because he doesn't want to deal with the different laws or changes that might affect him, converse with him about prenuptial agreements, and ensure him that things will only change for the better so that he can have a more positive outlook on what marriage can truly be.

183. Why does a man look at marriage as just a way to please a woman?

As explained in question #186, a lot of men are fine without marriage and would feel the same way about you whether married or not, so they might think of getting married as something that will just please you. A lot of women want that "happily ever after" relationship by becoming a wife to a husband, so it's easy for us to know that asking a woman that famous question "Will you marry me?" will please her in almost every way possible, especially when it's common for us to hear things like, "I want to get married" or "When are you going to ask me to marry you?" Another reason some men look at it as just a way to please a woman is because they don't feel as strongly as some women do about marriage. They can go through a relationship just fine without popping the question. So, men mainly do it to grant a woman's wishes since it's not that much of a wish for men as it is for women. Don't get me wrong—a lot of men want to get married, but it's just not that much of a need or priority as it is for women.

THE MALE TIP: If he's a guy who only wants to marry to please you, make sure he truly wants to get married to you because if not, it could backfire, and both of you could end up in a situation calling for divorce later down the line. Try asking him to write down a list of all the reasons why he wants to get married to make sure he's getting married for the right reasons.

184. Why might our relationship change after marriage, and how do I keep him interested?

It's sad to say, but I've read and heard about a ton of instances where couples have complained about their relationship changing after years of marriage and not in a good way, which is probably one of the reasons why divorce is common. From other people's experiences and from extensive research, it seems that once you're married, it brings on different expectations or stipulations than when you were just in a relationship. Priorities change such as the handling of children if any, making sure you're always 100 percent monogamous, and tending to each other may be a little more than before. So it seems natural for things to change, although it shouldn't be, but that change seems like it brings on more concerns or dissatisfactions rather than joy and contentment.

To keep him interested, just continue to perform the same way, and do the same things that interest him as you did before you were married.

THE MALE TIP: Try to keep the relationship fresh, meaning don't let it get so repetitious that it starts to become boring or predictable. If he becomes uninterested or you become concerned about whether he still is, do the same things you did while dating that pleased him and kept his interest. Try making it a priority to do those things regularly as much as possible, especially when he deserves it. Add a little more to your repertoire as well.

185. Why does he want to sign a prenuptial agreement?
He just wants to protect his assets, but it's possible that he wants yours to be protected as well. Some men think that having a prenuptial agreement is a safe and smart thing to do when getting married. It saves them from a lot of confusion, unnecessary arguments, and even stress during and after the divorce process. To avoid all the negativity on top of going through a divorce, it's good to sign a prenuptial agreement beforehand.

THE MALE TIP: Sign a prenuptial agreement to protect your assets, but if you feel it's not necessary, discuss your opinions with him, and let him know how you feel about it. If he wants one no matter what, think of it positively; don't think of it as being negative such as him not trusting that the marriage will last. Remember, it's mainly him wanting to avoid the headaches or confusion he might have to go through without one and being smart about his assets and maybe yours too.

186. Why doesn't he like the idea of having a traditional ceremony?
He may just want something different. He might feel that a traditional ceremony might not be as exciting or memorable as an untraditional one or that it's so common that he'd already know what to expect as if he'd been married before or seen it plenty of times. Some men prefer to keep things simple, and some like to go above and beyond.

THE MALE TIP: If he's not interested in having a traditional ceremony, try something different. Ask for his input on the type of wedding he prefers. If it's an issue where you want the traditional ceremony but he doesn't, you could try incorporating styles that both of you like into one ceremony. Discussing wedding plans is of paramount importance.

187. Why doesn't he believe in marriage or see it as important for a relationship?

As discussed earlier in this section, it's because he feels he can do the same type of things and feel the same type of way about his woman without marriage. This causes some men to question whether marriage is necessary, especially when some believe it won't be a significant change to the relationship as far as making it stronger. Your partner may not believe in marriage or see it as important because he fell in love before marriage and won't need it to fall in love again.

THE MALE TIP: Inform him about the importance of marriage by giving him positive and legitimate reasons as to why it is. No matter what a man believes, marriage is extremely important because of the lifelong commitment and the spiritual and emotional union two people get to experience.

35

Children

alking about having children is one of the touchiest subjects a couple can and will discuss. Some men don't want any, some men are up in the air about it, and some men don't mind having a bunch of them. There are men who fear having children or aren't ready to become a father, men who don't like children at all, and men who love the fatherhood life. There are so many different opinions and perceptions regarding how men feel about children and having them that it causes a ton of questions from women about it. It's a topic that should be discussed early in the relationship since it involves very important decisions and especially since it can either cut a relationship short or help it progress. Eventually you're going to need to discuss the topic with your partner, so you'll understand how he truly feels about having children. But until then, some of the most common questions are answered in this section to help you better understand men's actions and thoughts about having children, being a stepfather, and the rest of the fatherhood lifestyle.

188. Why doesn't he like kids?

Normally when a man doesn't like children, it's because he fears or hates the responsibilities that come with them such as having to monitor and discipline them, taking up personal time, caring for them, and so forth, or they're too much to deal with as far as their attitudes, actions, and sometimes the way they think. For example, some kids have slightly bad attitudes, some of them think that they're smarter and wiser than adults, and some of them try to walk, talk, and act like adults. Having to deal with those types of things can be stressful, which is why some men don't like dealing with kids or like them at all.

THE MALE TIP: You could try convincing him that kids aren't as hard to deal with as he may think. Give him a positive outlook about them; their attitudes, their actions, and the responsibilities that come with them.

189. Why doesn't he want children with me?

Maybe he doesn't like kids, he never wanted any of his own, or he doesn't see you as a fit mother. Perhaps, he feels that you, he, or both of you aren't ready for children, or he's not sure if the relationship will last. It could be any one or all these reasons why he doesn't want kids with you yet, but to sum it up, he isn't ready to have children with you because of his uncertainties.

THE MALE TIP: This is the perfect topic for a sit-down discussion with him. Ask him about his thoughts and feelings toward having children. Understand that there are a lot of factors we must consider before deciding on having kids, so be patient, don't force it, and do not get discouraged if you want it to happen but he doesn't because it may just be his thought now, and for sure this could change. If he doesn't want kids with you because of things like him not seeing you as a fit mother or doesn't think you're worthy, try to find ways that prove otherwise to make him more comfortable and sure that having a child with you isn't a bad decision. If he never wants kids and will never change, then you have some things to consider such as continuing with the relationship, whether you can go without having kids, or changing your thoughts about it.

190. Why does he say he's not ready to be a father when I know he'll do great?

He's either scared or unsure about being a father. Some men fear taking on the responsibilities fatherhood requires, and some men are unsure of themselves in terms of being a great loving father. For us, being a father is a huge responsibility, so there's a lot to think about before making a decision that affects our lives as well as the lives of others around us. Therefore, we need to be sure that we're fully ready and willing to take on those responsibilities.

THE MALE TIP: Be patient with him. Understand his feelings, and let him become ready on his own terms. Encourage him to be a great father.

191. Why did he act different or disappear after I told him I was pregnant?

Either getting you pregnant wasn't his intention or it was his intention, but he's not ready to take on the responsibilities of being a father. Disappearing or acting different is his way of saying he doesn't want a child or that he's scared out of his mind about being a father. Whether he feels it's not the right time, he's not ready, you're not the right person, or it was a mistake, it all comes down to him not really wanting a child or not wanting to have the responsibilities it entails. The worst-case scenario is that he disappears with plans of disowning the child, but no matter the reason, they're all sad. Some men will purposely get a woman pregnant to try to stay in her life forever although they have no intentions of taking care of the child.

THE MALE TIP: If he begins to act differently, express how you feel about it. Also, discuss and figure out what's best for both of you in terms of keeping the child or not. Although abortion is unjust, some people have to consider it. If it's a situation where he's scared of becoming a father, encourage him that he'll be fine. If he disappears from your life, then do what you need to do as far as getting prepared to be a single mother, taking care of those parenting duties without him.

192. Why doesn't he call to check on his kid? (Case of separated parents)

It depends on the type of father he is or the type of relationship they have together, and sometimes it depends on the type of relationship you and the father have together. Of course, there are different types of fathers. He could be the type who feels like his kid is in good hands with you, and therefore he doesn't think he needs to check on him or doesn't think it's a big deal, especially if he sees the child every so often. He could be the type of father who doesn't care to do such things. He could be so tied up in his own personal life that he forgets. It's also possible that he doesn't call to avoid having to deal with you, which is sometimes the case for some parents. But no matter what the reason is, it's safe to say that a father should call to check on his child because it matters to the child.

THE MALE TIP: If it's an issue that's affecting the child, be sure to communicate that with the child's father. Remember that you can't really control other people's actions, but you can advise them to do what's right. If he doesn't call, and no one cares or is affected by it, then don't worry yourself about it.

193. Why does he still want kids when I already have enough of my own?

He's probably the family-man type and wants a lot of kids, or he wants kids of his own bloodline by you. Although you have kids who aren't biologically his, it doesn't mean that they're his kids just because you're in a relationship with him. Yes, he may be involved in their lives abundantly, maybe even more than their biological father, but to a lot of men in these situations, there are still certain rules and regulations that they have to abide by since they aren't their actual father. It's basically a level of respect that should be shown to the child and the child's biological father as far as how he treats and disciplines the child. Some men prefer to handle and raise a child as they see fit, which is a reason why they'd rather have kids of their own. Of course, he can still raise your children the way that he sees fit, but there will always be limitations, and don't forget the common phrase: there's nothing like having your own.

THE MALE TIP: Find out how important it is for him to have his own children. If he feels that it's a necessity or feels strongly about it, consider giving it to him. If you truly don't want any more, explain why, and maybe he'll consider your feelings. If both of you can't come up with an agreement, you may need to consider moving on.

194. Why does he treat his kid differently, sometimes better than he treats mine?

A lot of men tend to do this, and it can be explained by saying that some men might not feel as responsible for another guy's child as for his own. Yes, he's still responsible for your child if you're in a relationship with him, but normally in those situations, it's to a certain degree. For example, he may not try to enroll your child in sports or teach your child how to ride a bike because the biological father might want to be the one responsible for those types of things. Most biological fathers who are involved in their child's life want to be the only male involved or responsible for such things, which may cause your partner to step back a bit although it may cause him to look as if he's treating his own child better than yours if he's only involved in those types of things with his child. If it's a situation where your child's biological father isn't around and your partner still acts this way, it may be accidental since we all have a tendency of being more involved with our own children than someone else's. The worst-case scenario is that he does it purposely just because the child isn't his.

THE MALE TIP: Inform him of your concern especially if it feels biased against your child. Understand that it may be accidental and out of habit of people treating their own things better than someone else's. Also, make sure he recognizes the differences of how he treats each child so that he'll know what to change.

195. Why doesn't he feel comfortable disciplining my kid?
Although he's considered a father figure and in your child's life, he may not know how comfortable you or the biological father feels about him disciplining your child. I've been in a situation personally where I've dated a woman long term who had a child, and the moment I decided to discipline her child, it ended up coming off as too aggressive although she was a witness of me disciplining my own child in a similar manner numerous times. Before then I was slightly uncomfortable about disciplining her child for that particular

reason. Also, some men believe that a level of respect should be shown toward the child and the child's biological father since most men prefer to be the only male disciplining their child in certain manners. Sort of like a bro code.

THE MALE TIP: If you want or need him to discipline your child, express that to him, but make sure his ways of disciplining are acceptable and respectable. Try having a sit-down with him and the biological father to come to an agreement on how to raise and discipline the child so there won't be any issues between anyone.

Part Seven

TO BE OR NOT TO BE: Questions and Answers about Spending Quality Time, Long-Distance Relationships, Your Female Friends, Dating Others, Second Chances, and Breakups

36

Quality Time

Quality time is defined as time spent in giving another person one's undivided attention to strengthen a relationship. In the book *The Five Love Languages,* Gary Chapman describes quality time as an important expression of love and focused attention. Although spending time with each other is a mutual effort in relationships, sometimes the male and female versions of what it is differ. Some men consider quality time to be something as simple as sitting at home watching television together, which involves little or no effort. And some women don't think it's enough to be considered quality time. Is it because women crave more time and effort than men, and therefore they expect more than just being around each other to be consider quality time? Whether we think differently than women or not about

what's considered quality time, it's a normal issue in relationships. A lot of us forget how important it is to spend time
with our partner and how important it is for our relationship to flourish, and because of it, questions or concerns are
constantly expressed and overthought regarding it.

196. What does a man consider to be quality time in a relationship?

Quality time for a man is giving his woman as much of his
time and attention as he possibly can. Sometimes it's sacri-
ficing other things in his life to dedicate more of his time to
you. It may differ a bit from man to man; some men consider
things such as sitting on the couch watching TV together to be
quality time, and some consider it to be something as simple
as having a five-minute conversation with you. Regardless of
the simplicity of events, a man's quality time can be anything
that involves his undivided attention no matter the length of
time.

THE MALE TIP: Understand that a man's quality time can be
any time spent with you doing anything if you have his undivided attention.

197. Why doesn't he like to spend as much quality time as I do, and does it mean he doesn't love me?

It's probably safe to say that women in relationships have the
tendency to want all or most of their man's time, which is
hard for us to give being that we're so busy trying to make
sure we're taking care of business like we're supposed to. I'm

WHY MEN THIS, WHY MEN THAT?

not saying women don't need the same amount of time to do such things, but women seem to be able to manage better and give more time to their man, which is one of the reasons why it will seem like we don't like spending as much quality time as women. Most of the time, it's not that we don't like to do; it's more so because we can't. You should also realize that some men think spending too much time together is a bit mushy, too sentimental, and a lot of them would rather not be seen in such a way, especially by their male friends, but it doesn't have anything to do with him not loving you.

THE MALE TIP: Understand that it's just a man thing, but if you feel that he doesn't spend enough quality time with you, express it. I'm sure he'll understand and try to give you the time you need.

198. Why does he constantly make excuses about spending time with me?

This means that he doesn't care to spend time with you, the things that you want him to do don't interest him, or he truly doesn't have time to spend. Although there are a few reasons why we constantly make excuses to not spend time with our partner, it's mainly because we just don't feel like doing anything, which could also be an excuse in itself.

THE MALE TIP: Let him know if you feel like he makes too many excuses when it comes to spending time with you. There's nothing wrong with wanting to spend a lot of time with your partner because strong, lasting, and pleasurable

197

relationships are sometimes built on how well a couple spends their time together.

199. Why doesn't he like to cuddle?

This depends on the male. Some men don't like to cuddle because it's not comfortable enough for them, and some men don't like the physical attention it involves as much as some women do. We all know that cuddling is more of a woman's thing although men like to cuddle at times as well and are sometimes the first to initiate it, but it just seems more of a woman's nature to want or need it regularly. It can also have little to do with the fact that it's not viewed by some men as macho, and some men would rather adhere to that macho mentality or have a macho personality.

THE MALE TIP: Only thing that you could really do is to continue to initiate the first contact when you want to cuddle. You can't really force a guy to suddenly enjoy cuddling if he doesn't care for it. Just appreciate the times he does.

200. Why does he hang out with his friends more than he does with me?

This is a common complaint among women. It could be that whatever he and his friends do is normally more exciting or interesting than the things you do together. Another possibility is that he and his friends can talk about things that he doesn't feel comfortable talking to you about. Also, don't forget that living with him might influence it as well. For example, he might not be as attentive to go out and do things with you being that he lives with you and sees you regular-ly, which sometimes makes a man more prone to planning things with his friends instead of with you.

THE MALE TIP: Express your concern about the issue to him. Tell him how it makes you feel, especially since this issue can negatively affect your relationship.

37

Long-Distance Relationships

I'm sure a lot of us agree that long-distance relation-ships can be extremely hard to maintain. One reason is that you just never know what the other individual is up to. You're basically putting your trust into someone whom you'll rarely see or be able to spend time with un-less it's under some type of twenty-first-century technology such as FaceTime, Skype, or Snapchat. In addition to not knowing what the other person is up to, there are so many other things that you must go through to make it work. For example, you'll eventually have to worry about things such as who's going to relocate to live with each other, when will the relocation take place, what he does in his free time while you're away and vice versa, and what's next after someone fi-nally relocates. Those types of things can be very worrisome, if they're not already, and could also be the reason for doubt-ing whether the relationship will work or last. Here are a few questions that I'm sure are very familiar when dealing with a long-distance relationship.

201. Why is it hard for him to believe that I'm being loyal from afar?

This can be hard for anyone who's in a long-distance re-lationship to believe, not just him. When dating long dis-tance, it's easier to make the wrong decisions as far as not fully respecting your relationship being that your partner is so many miles away, and he can't be there during times of need like when you're lonely, aroused, missing him, and so forth. A lot of us know this, and it sometimes causes us to not feel as confident as we should be about being in a loyal and trustworthy relationship; also, temptation seems to con-quer both males and females these days. It's not rare to hear about a long-distance relationship failing because of infi-delity issues, so it's hard for some men to expect the opposite. Finally, there could've been something you've done or told him that gave him the impression that you wouldn't be loyal in a long-distance relationship.

THE MALE TIP: Show and remind him often of your loyalty to-ward him, especially if he's a man with trust issues. Continue to make the right decisions that are best for the relationship, and if his negative thoughts are taking a toll on you and the relationship, you may need to consider taking a break from the relationship.

202. Why does he act different toward me, especially more nervous, when I finally get around him from being miles apart?

It's pretty much the same as when a woman's been talking on the phone with a guy that she misses, cares about, whom she talks to about anything and everything, but as soon as she gets around him, she becomes so excited that she acts differently. She might act nervous, scared, or anxious simply because she's so ecstatic to see him and has been waiting patiently. Men act the same way when it comes to women. It's safe to say that everyone has experienced those types of feelings at some point or another during his or her lifetime, especially at a young age when dating begins. Shyness may play a role in it as well. If it's an instance where he shows more rudeness than ever before, it's probably been his personality all along, he just never displays it until he's around you, or he just doesn't know how to act around you and loses himself, meaning he forgets who he is.

THE MALE TIP: Since it may be a natural thing for some, try not to worry about it. Welcome his nervousness because he may just be super excited to finally be around you. If he's being rude and it puts some sort of a damper on your feelings toward him, try to bring it up in a respectable manner. Tell him to be himself always.

203. Why does he constantly call to check on me more than normal?

Either he loves and misses you or he doesn't trust you. If he does it because he loves or misses you, then he calls to hear your voice or for conversation. If he does it because he doesn't trust you, then he's doing it to make sure you're not doing anything that you aren't supposed to be doing that could hurt his feelings or damage the relationship. It's like a man's way of spying on you.

THE MALE TIP: Try not to pay it any mind, but if it's bothersome or annoying or you feel like you aren't given any space because he calls too much, express it to him. If he does it because he misses you, try to give him the benefit of the doubt by being fond of it and patient with him until it becomes excessive.

204. Why does he think I call him too much or not enough?
If he thinks you call him too much, then it's probably something personal with him. Maybe he's never heard of a woman calling as much as you do, or he's just not used to it. There are plenty of reasons why a man might think a woman calls him too much, but it's a question that only the source can answer because of the many possibilities. One reason why he might think you don't call enough is because he probably thinks that a woman is supposed to call at certain times such as in the morning, at least once during the day, and before bed. If you don't call regularly during those times, it will make him feel like you don't call enough. Otherwise, it could be if he only hears from you once a day because a lot of men think that once isn't enough for long-distance relationships. There are plenty of other possible reasons regarding this issue that should only be answered by the individual involved.

THE MALE TIP: The only true way to find out how he feels is to ask him since there are a lot of different reasons why he might think that you call him too much or don't call enough.

205. Why does he think I should be the one to relocate?

Simply because he's the male and it's normal for women to be the ones who relocate for their partner. It could also have to do with him possibly having a better career or living situation where he's at than where you are or even a better place as far as the country or state he resides. He could also expect you to relocate depending on whether it was his idea in the first place, but today it's just common for the woman to relocate for the man.

THE MALE TIP: Weigh out the pros and cons of you relocating, and then compare it to his to figure out what's the best logical decision. If he wants you to relocate although it might not be the smartest decision, consider it, and think about all your options. Always have a backup plan if the relationship after the relocation doesn't work out. If you don't see yourself making the decision to relocate for him, try convincing him to, and if no one agrees, you may need to consider moving on relationship-wise. Remember what's important to you, and to accomplish things, you must learn to take risks no matter the drawbacks. Take all that into consideration.

206. Why does he constantly believe that the relationship won't work?

It's hard to believe that any long-distance relationship will work especially since they're known not to last. He might not trust you, or he might think that no one will truly want to relocate for the other. Since so many things are tied into long-distance relationships, so many things are a cause for worry, worry causes negative thoughts, and negative thoughts cause negative energy, all of these will reflect on the belief—the belief that the relationship won't last. Long-distance relationships can be very difficult to maintain, and not many people expect the unexpected. In fact, most people expect those relationships to be temporary.

THE MALE TIP: Surround the relationship with only positive energy, and continue to be optimistic for a long-lasting relationship. Also, avoid as much negative energy toward the relationship as possible because negative energy and worry are some of the ingredients for failed relationships.

38

Your Female Friends

A man knows how important your female friends can be to you and how they can influence the way you think, act, and even what mood you're in. Although some women don't get along with other women or prefer not to have female friends, I'd say many women are the opposite, or it depends on age. Is it true that a woman always has at least one lady companion to discuss certain things with or spend time with every so often? Whether it's true or not, a lot of men think that's the case because women seem to always have that one friend or family member they gossip with 24-7. The fact that women love gossiping causes some men to think that it influences what a woman feels or thinks about them being that men are a lot of times the focus of some of their conversations. It also causes some men to have a lot of negative opinions toward your friends, even disliking them, depending on what your topics of discussion are. Although a man shouldn't have to get in between what you decide to do and discuss with your friends, a lot of them are known to do so, and it causes women to have a lot of questions about how a man acts and feels regarding their friends.

207. Why doesn't he like me gossiping to my friends about him or our relationship?

He doesn't want anyone in his business, making comments, discussing it with other people, or using it to his or her advantage. There are so many problems that can arise from you gossiping about your partner or your relationship that men would rather avoid this. Usual problems are that your friends make inappropriate or false comments about certain things that could potentially influence you to have the same outlook or the conversation ends up circulating to others allowing them to be able to spread false information known as rumors. Issues like these are common from gossip, and I'm sure it's the main reason why he doesn't like you gossiping to your friends about him and your relationship.

THE MALE TIP: Avoid gossiping about things pertaining to him and your relationship to your friends. We know that you may do it to relieve stress, or you just need someone to talk to and get things off your chest, but choose wisely what you decide to discuss with your friends. Certain things shouldn't be discussed with friends.

208. Why does he act so unnecessarily nice to my friends?
He's just being polite and wants to get in good standing with
them. Some men know how beneficial it can be to have a positive, friendly relationship with your friends especially since
friends will sometimes have an influence on you and your
decisions. He probably wants to make sure that your friends
have nothing but good things to say about him so that you
have a positive outlook about him as your partner. Some men
also act nice to develop a friendly relationship with them in
hopes of getting the inside scoop on some of your endeavors
or whatever else your friends might be willing to tell. The
worst-case scenario of him acting unnecessarily nice is because he's flirting with the wrong intentions, to maybe hook
up with them.

THE MALE TIP: Let him be friendly toward your friends because it truly is a positive thing to have people you're around
regularly approve of the guy you're dating, but address it if
it's getting out of hand.

209. Why does he act like his friends are better than mine?
This depends on the way he thinks. One reason is that he
might not like your friends, so he acts like his are better to
belittle yours. Another reason is that he might not like you
hanging out with them, so he plays some sort of comparison
game to make it seem like his friends are the type of people
you should want to hang around, not yours. A third reason is
that he tries to make himself look like a better, more knowledgeable person than you, which he does by way of comparing

WHY MEN THIS, WHY MEN THAT?

the type of people you've befriended and the type of people he's befriended as if his circle of friends is much better than yours. There are other reasons why he might act this way, but it's mainly based on his character.

THE MALE TIP: Explain to him that regardless of whose friends he thinks are of better character, it's not fair to compare such things. It creates negativity that can have an effect on everyone involved, including you.

210. Why doesn't he like my friends even though they're always nice toward him and have no problems with him?
He could be the type of guy who doesn't like dealing with a woman's friends or doesn't like for you to have any association with them for whatever reason. As explained earlier in this section, since female friends can have so much influence on a woman, some men automatically stamp them as people they don't like whether they're nice or not, maybe because they've had bad experiences with those types of friends. There could also be situations that he wants to avoid that might happen because of your friends, and he does it by letting you know that he doesn't like them—and also to try to make you minimize your association with them.

THE MALE TIP: Try discussing the situation with him, and explain that it's unnecessary to dislike someone for such reasons when they're nothing but positive and nice toward him. But understand that him disliking someone is his choice, and he has every right to make his own decisions. Keep the peace by limiting the amount of time you bring your friends around him.

211. What would he think about my friend living with us?

Some men think that it's perfectly fine, and some think that it's not a very good idea. I can tell you that inviting another woman into your home is not always a good idea being that there are so many incidents that could happen that could affect your relationship, such as him and your friend becoming too close to each other developing a want for each other, him becoming annoyed if your friend begins to be in too much of his or your own personal space, or from certain rules you might have set for your household that aren't being followed, and so forth. There are many possibilities that could cause a rocky relationship between everyone involved when allowing another woman to live in the household. I would only recommend it if your friend doesn't have anywhere else to go or if you trust everyone involved to handle it like adults by abiding by household rules and respecting each other's space and privacy, but you'll never really know what goes through a man's mind when you mention one of your friends coming to stay. It also depends on everyone's maturity level because it shouldn't be a problem.

THE MALE TIP: Discuss it with him to get an idea of how he feels about it.

39

Dating Others

When a man's ex-girlfriend decides to date other men, it can be an emotional situation for him. His feelings about it become exposed, jealousy begins to transpire, and the whole thought of you moving on might become painful for him. Let's be honest—no one really likes for someone he or she loved to go searching for another love interest especially when you've had an excellent relationship together. For men, they might not act like their ex moving on bothers them, but in all reality, a lot of times it does. Some men even go as far as trying to tell a woman that she'll never find another like him; or they'll only look to date a woman who has similar or the exact same qualities as their ex. Although a man might tell you time and time again to move on as if he won't be bothered by you doing so, the truth is that it can bother him, and he'll act in ways that cause you to wonder why he didn't just become the guy whom you needed instead of allowing you to move on.

212. Why does he tell me I'll never find another like him?
Either he believes it, or he's only saying it to convince you that he's the best you've ever had to keep you around. If he believes that the men you've dated in the past don't amount to him or that your future partners won't either, he'll say it to make you believe the same. We're notorious for saying it during certain arguments or when our woman threatens to leave us. I'd say it's mainly used as a tactic so that you'll rethink dating another man.

THE MALE TIP: Ignore those types of statements if you consider them to be untrue. Understand that it's mainly said as a tactic, and no man truly knows whether you'll find a better man—it's just something that we say or try to scare you with.

213. Why is it so hard for him to be the guy whom I need instead of dating someone else?
Normally when a woman has this problem, it's because a man is stuck in his ways and doesn't seem to understand or want to understand what she wants from him. Also, when a woman tries to change certain things about a man that he doesn't know how to or doesn't want to change, it can make it seem like he isn't the guy whom she needs, or there could be too much expectation placed on him. Or he wasn't meant to be the guy you need.

THE MALE TIP: Let him be the person who he is. Try not to give him such high expectations. Only suggest him to change certain things for you—don't force him to do so. If he continues to be the guy whom you don't need, consider moving on.

214. Does he really think he'll find someone better, with better qualities?

He may or may not. If he does, it's because he believes that the qualities you've showed him aren't hard to replace, or he might think that you aren't the woman for him if those qualities don't make him happy. If he doubts finding someone better but says he will, it's just another tactic used to scare you or make you believe he's serious, or maybe he hopes he'll find that someone.

THE MALE TIP: If he's important to you, try becoming the woman whom he needs, and do what makes him happy. If he tells you such things but it's not how he truly feels, simply ignore that type of statements because they don't hold any weight. It's sometimes just something men say, sometimes out of anger, although there still may be some truth to it.

215. Why did he try to date a woman with similar qualities as me?

To make you jealous, or maybe he loved your qualities, so he wants to date the same type of woman. If a man does it to make you jealous, it's sort of his way of saying, "I can easily go out and get another just like you," but if he does it because he loved the qualities you possessed, it normally means that those qualities made him happy and is his ideal type of woman.

THE MALE TIP: Remember that it's his choice to date whomever he wants. Try not to comment or display any type of jealousy or concern toward him dating another woman with similar qualities as you. Ask yourself whether it really matters.

40

Second Chances

Giving a man a second chance in a relationship could either be beneficial or not. Some men take advantage of the opportunity while some men are undeserving as if nothing is going to change. If you've ever given a guy a second chance, then you should know exactly what I'm talking about. However, if you haven't, you will begin to understand the moment you decide to give him a second chance. The difference with certain men is that some tend to change for the better and begin to become everything you've always wanted, trying to correct all the mistakes that didn't sit well with you. Then there are the men who put you in a position that causes you to question whether a second chance was even worth your time, and it is those types of men whom I focus on in this section. They tend to treat you differently, meaning they don't put much effort into the relationship as they used to. They tend to hide the fact that they're still involved with the same women whom they were dealing with while both of you were on a hiatus, but at the same time, they expect you to drop everything you had going on to focus on them, and these types of actions are displayed often by many men.

216. Why does he treat me differently than the last time we dated?

If he treats you better than before, he might have just become a better person, or he might feel that the way he used to treat you was the reason for the breakup. He wants to show you how good of a man he can and should be.

If he doesn't treat you as well as he used to, he may have lost a bit of feelings for you, or he feels like he put a lot of effort into you and the relationship but wasn't appreciated. He may not care about the relationship as much as he used, as if he's somewhat drained or tired of trying so hard.

THE MALE TIP: Address it if it's affecting the relationship now. Understand that people will change for the better or worse, so you shouldn't expect someone to be the same as he was in the past. Sometimes things change when you go back to dating a guy from the past.

217. Why doesn't he take me out as much as he did when we first dated?

He may not feel it's necessary anymore. Men sometimes get comfortable in relationships and stop doing some of the things that they used to do for their woman that would impress her. For example, in the beginning of the relationship, he might do things like open your car door for you, send you flowers, or take you out on dates regularly, but after a while he gets comfortable and sort of feels like he already accomplished what he needed to, and those types of things either stop or diminish. It happens with a lot of men and is a common complaint among a lot of women.

THE MALE TIP: Remind him to not stop doing the things that he used to do that made you happy. Understand that it's a common issue and we just need to be reminded. We truly do get comfortable and stop doing certain things.

218. Will he ever go back to the amazing guy I used to know?

It's possible, but you never know. It all depends on him, but if he's a guy of good character, then I believe he will, although it may take some time.

THE MALE TIP: Express how you feel, but be patient, and don't have high hopes in expecting him to. Let him go back to being that amazing guy on his own terms.

219. Am I going to have to accept women calling his phone from when we were broken up?

Yes, but only for a little while. Obviously while you guys were broken up, he probably was out dating, exchanging numbers, and so forth, so you shouldn't expect all the phone calls from other women to immediately stop when you start back dating him. Out of respect he should stop seeing and conversing with other women, but he doesn't have full control over when a woman decides to call, especially if she doesn't know his current situation.

THE MALE TIP: Do not get discouraged when you see a woman calling his phone. Give it time to die down before you start insisting him to do things like change his number. If it's still happening after too long, address it because it shouldn't be happening.

220. Why doesn't he want to get rid of his lady fling although I'm giving him a second chance at a relationship between us?

He's probably waiting to make sure your second chance is worth it, or he cares for her enough to not want to get rid of her. If he doesn't want to get rid of her because you and him just started dating again, it could be because he wants to make sure he's not getting rid of someone just for a temporary relationship with you. In a way, you could call it insurance in case you and he don't work out. But if he keeps her around although she's a problem, then he cares about her or enjoys their liaisons.

THE MALE TIP: If he doesn't want to get rid of her because you just started dating him, give it some time to make sure he knows that you're serious about a long-term relationship with him. Once he knows that, he should voluntarily dismiss her from his life. If he's the type who wants to have his cake and eat it too, meaning he wants to be involved with you and another woman, then there will be some things that you must consider such as continuing with the relationship or not. But in all reality, having more than one woman is unacceptable unless it's just a friend, and to some women, even that's unacceptable.

221. Why does he expect me to just drop everything and be all about him now that I've given him a second chance? It's common for a man to expect this, but it's basically a pride and respect thing; he wants to be the only man who has your attention. When a woman drops everything for a man, it shows that she cares and respects him and the situation, which is probably what he wants to see. Some men only expect a woman to do so if he's the controlling self-centered type and wants everything to be about him. He could also expect it to see how serious you are about being in a relationship with him, or he wants to jump right into things and act as if you guys were never broken up.

THE MALE TIP: If you feel comfortable dropping everything for him, do so. If you don't, explain to him why, and hopefully he'll understand. If he doesn't understand or wants to be selfish about it, maybe consider giving him what he wants, or just do what you want, but eventually you'll have to come to an agreement regarding the issue.

41

Breaking Up

reaking up is the end of an era—an era that a person either cherished or despised. We all know that it can happen for numerous reasons. For example, a guy not thinking you're good enough for him, financial issues, control issues, infidelity issues, and probably the most common of them all: poor communication and small-minded arguments. No matter what the reason is, a breakup is not a good experience for anyone involved who was in a loving and caring relationship. For many, breakups cause sadness and heartbreak, but some people are gladdened by their breakup if they feel like it was a relief or weight off their shoulders, but it all depends on the type of relationship the person was involved in, whether good, bad, stressful, abusive, and so forth. What's somewhat bizarre about some breakups is that whether good or bad, some men think that women should still abide by certain rules although they're not together anymore. For example, not dating or conversing with other men too soon and thinking they should still be involved in that woman's life in one way or another simply because they have history together, but this has something to do with a man's ego and whether he thinks there's a chance to get back together. In this section I discuss some of the things women question the most such as why a man will break up over something so stupid, why it's so hard for some men to work things out, and one of the most famous issues of all: constantly making up and breaking up.

222. Why does he allow us to break up over something so stupid like a petty argument?

That petty argument might be considered a major problem in his mind, or the arguing alone is an issue that he doesn't want in a relationship. Some men are extremely annoyed or disappointed by petty arguments, and they'll go as far as breaking up with a woman to avoid them. Sometimes it's only done out of anger, so it's a reaction, not a well-planned decision. For some men, it's even a habit to break up with a woman after arguing or fighting, but be cautious if it's done excessively because it could be a sign of controlling behavior by trying to threaten you with a breakup to get you to do certain things or act a certain way.

THE MALE TIP: Tell him how it makes you feel and how it might affect the relationship, or you could go as far as seeking couples counseling if it becomes a serious problem. Don't allow anyone to constantly break up with you especially after arguments because worrying about the next time he's going to break up with you because of an argument can take a toll on your mind, body, and spirit.

223. Why does he think I wasn't good enough?

You probably didn't meet his expectations or standards of the type of woman he wanted. For example, he may have felt like your status in life as far as your job, accomplishments, and so forth weren't up to par with his, your work ethic wasn't at a level he was satisfied with, your overall outlook toward life didn't coincide with his, the things that you liked to do weren't of the same class as his, or he thinks that you didn't do enough for him. Although these things may sound absurd, they're all things that could make some people believe that another person isn't good enough for them. But in all actuality, you are good no matter what anyone else thinks.

THE MALE TIP: Understand that when a man thinks this way, it's normally a personal issue within himself. Never believe that you aren't good enough for anyone because you are who you are, and you are who you're made to be. If he didn't like you for you, he shouldn't have been someone you were involved with.

224. Why doesn't he want me dating or talking to other guys right after the breakup?

He could be trying to make sure there's an opportunity for him to get back with you, without having to deal with or worry about other guys in the picture. It could be his way of trying to have a bit of control over you, or he may just be the jealous type. A lot of men don't like when a woman moves on and dates other men too quickly after you've broken up because there's always a chance you may get back together soon after, and it makes some men feel like they were easy to replace or that their ex didn't care enough about them to give it time.

THE MALE TIP: If you think there's a chance you might get back together, try to avoid dating or talking to other men because it could make things difficult. If you don't care about what he thinks or whether you'll get back together, feel free to do as you please, but try to be patient when it comes to dating other men because moving too fast could cause you to make the wrong decisions.

225. Why does he act like it's a problem to work things out?

Maybe it is a problem, or maybe he's playing hardball or is arrogant. If it's a problem, he may be tired of the relationship and feel like he's had enough and that it just doesn't work, especially if you guys tried making it work numerous times. If he knows you want to work things out but he's playing hardball or acting arrogant, then he's only causing you to go through emotions to maybe get what he wants out of you—sort of his way of using it to his advantage. Some men even demand ultimatums before they start acting civil about trying to make the relationship work.

THE MALE TIP: If he doesn't prefer to stay and work things out, don't force him to because it could result in an unhealthy relationship or a relationship that you're constantly trying to prove yourself. Although some women have had progress forcing a man to stay, I still wouldn't recommend doing so. If you've been the one at fault for the breakup, and you don't want him to go anywhere, I'd try to explain to him the things you could change to make for a better, more desirable relationship. Also, don't play into his mind games if his intentions aren't to make things work.

226. Would things have turned out differently if I would have done better?

It would've or it wouldn't. If he had his mind made up about what he wanted out of the relationship regardless of the kind of woman you were to him, then it probably wouldn't have mattered if you were to do better. It all depends on the type of guy he is, the intentions he had, and the type of relationship he wanted. But if he wanted the relationship but a lot of problems persisted in it, then things probably could've been different if those problems would have improved.

THE MALE TIP: Explain to him that you're willing to do better. I'd also suggest giving him space to see if he comes back around. You could try pursuing him, but make sure you capitalize on the opportunity by being and doing the best you can if the relationship is given another chance.

227. Why does it seem like we break up just to make up?

This is one of the most common issues within relationships and happens to just about everyone. It doesn't mean that your relationship is on the brink of failure or that it isn't restorable; it just means that you're trying to figure each other out and getting each other to understand what will be acceptable and unacceptable in the relationship. When couples break up, a lot of times, it's because of a simple disagreement that wasn't accepted or understood at the time, and making up is a way of saying "It's okay. Apology accepted. Try not to let it happen again." The reason it's a common occurrence is because there's so much to learn about a person and what they will and won't accept, and a lot of people don't just sit down and talk about those types of things like responsible adults; instead, they end up arguing about it or playing mind games by testing a person's limits and end up overreacting by breaking up with his or her partner when things aren't going right. So, if it seems like you break up to make up, just think of it as both of you trying to figure things and each other out.

THE MALE TIP: Talk things out instead of breaking up. You could even make a rule with each other such as you must try to work things out before deciding to end the relationship. But don't make breaking up and making up a habit because it might eventually get to a point where you never make up.

About the Author

Lloyd Johnson III was born in the city of St. Louis, Missouri, where he spent the first eleven years of his life. It wasn't until the age of twelve that he developed a deep interest in literature. Ever since, his interest has turned into a passion unquestionably. He also has a passion for people as well as helping them get accurate advice about life's lessons. Accurate information is so paramount to him and his writings that he eventually gave birth to the phrase "If it isn't right, I shall not write."

He studied business while taking writing courses at the St. Louis Community College—Meramec campus. He's developed relationships with hundreds of different people throughout the United States by way of travel and social media, which has given him the opportunity to hear and be a part of numerous amounts of life stories from different ethnicities and personalities all over. His experiences and studies throughout those relationships have also given him the knowledge and ability to give fact-based information and advice about life and relationships to others in need, mainly women.

Lloyd is a proud father of one daughter, a loving family man, and an overall civil human being. He takes pride in his work, and it shows.

Ljlj314@yahoo.com

Suggested Titles That May Interest You

Alexis, Sabrina and Charles, Eric. *10 Things Every Woman Needs to Know About Men: Understand His Mind and Capture His Heart.* CreateSpace Publishing, 2015.

Harvey, Steve. *Act Like a Lady, Think Like a Man.; What Men Really Think about Love, Relationships, Intimacy, and Commitment.* New York: HarperCollins, 2010.

Harvey, Steve. *Straight Talk, No Chaser: How to Find, Keep, and Understand a Man.* New York: Amistad, 2012.

Hussey, Matthew. *Get the Guy: Learn Secrets of the Male Mind to Find the Man You Want and the Love You Deserve.* New York: Harperwave, 2014.

Michaelsen, Gregg. *To Date a Man, You Must Understand a Man: The Keys to Catch a Great Guy.* CreateSpace Independent Pub., 2014.

Share Your Thoughts

If there is anything mentioned in this book that you do not believe or agree with, want more information or a more thorough explanation about a particular topic or question, or just want to share your thoughts or comments, please feel free to contact me. I'd love to hear it.

To contact me, write to this address:

Lloyd Johnson III
P.O. Box 511
Wentzville, MO 63385

Or you can reach me by e-mail at LjLj314@yahoo.com

www.ingramcontent.com/pod-product-compliance
Lightning Source LLC
LaVergne TN
LVHW051255080426
835509LV00020B/2988